Georgette, Where Are You?

And Other Stories of God
Interacting with His People

CHARLOTTE POTEET

WESTBOW
PRESS®
A DIVISION OF THOMAS NELSON
& ZONDERVAN

WestBow Press books may be ordered through booksellers or by contacting:

WestBow Press
A Division of Thomas Nelson & Zondervan
1663 Liberty Drive
Bloomington, IN 47403
www.westbowpress.com
1 (866) 928-1240

ISBN: 978-1-5127-7988-2 (sc)
ISBN: 978-1-5127-7990-5 (hc)
ISBN: 978-1-5127-7989-9 (e)

Library of Congress Control Number: 2017904319

Print information available on the last page.

WestBow Press rev. date: 03/23/2017

You have given me
the heritage
of those
who fear your name.

(Psalm 61:5)

Contents

Acknowledgments

For my original family, I give thanks to God. I am greatly indebted to my parents and my older brother for the ways they taught me to think about God and to recognize Him as the most important thing in life. I will thank them in person when I see them again in heaven. I am also thankful for the grandparents, aunts, uncles, and cousins to whom I am much indebted.

I can say with complete certainty that not the first thing would have been done toward publishing this book without the faithful and constant support of my husband, Bill. He is the godly force behind our daily lives, always looking toward Jesus, "the author and finisher of our faith," as the Bible says. He has not only encouraged me to write, but has also spent untold hours editing, formatting, and sweating through details that would have ended everything if it had been left up to me.

I must acknowledge my dear cousin, Billie Holladay, who has been the final impetus which drove me to compile these collected stories and publish them, for it was never my intent to do this. Her enthusiasm and gentle insistence was what put me over the top, so to speak—but only with the hope that these various accounts would encourage those individuals who read them.

Another cousin I must acknowledge is Jean Robertson, a lifetime friend and spiritual mentor, and the one who exhorted me to pray and to trust God in all things. We shared the family stories and laughed and cried together for all the time we had in this life. She resides now with her Lord Jesus, and I miss her terribly—but only for a season.

My son, James, who also loves to write, has always encouraged me and has given a great deal of practical advice and counsel. He has also enabled my husband and me to stay current with technology—the tools of writing. My nephew, Rob Russell, has encouraged me and has read some of these stories with the eye of an accountant, which makes me think they might have a broader audience than just my close friends.

A host of friends have read some of the stories and have been very supportive. I treasure each of them for their very specific ways of encouragement (alphabetically): Tony and Tammy Bellusci, Therese Bocchino, Joan Houghton, Ruth Koch, Gail Loken, Jayne Mattocks, Phyllis Olsen, Florea Sansing, Margaret Smith, and Jo Rita Vinyard.

Without people to hear stories, there would be no point to tell stories. I must acknowledge the children of the past and the present who listened to my stories and urged me on with the cheerful call to "tell me a story!" My love to Jody, Polly, George, Alese, Marty, Beth, Olivia, Jordan, Matthew, Ruth, Abbie, Audra, and Meredith.

I am thankful for each member of the team at Westbow Press, for the kindness and skill that has elevated the quality of this endeavor to a far better product. For an artist who can reach into the imagination of another person and express just what was envisioned, and for an editor who can correct and alter, without compromising, the tone of the book, I say a heartfelt thank you.

I am especially grateful for the people who shared their stories and let me have a glimpse of the ways God has been a part of their daily lives. Also many friends at the New Salem Baptist Church.

Above all, I am grateful to God for allowing me the pleasure of writing and giving me an eye to see Him at work in the life of every person.

An Opening Word to the Reader

$\mathcal{I}$ come from a family of storytellers. Many Saturday nights in my early childhood were spent in the little farmhouse of my aunt and uncle, who were tenant farmers—poor in the world's goods, but rich indeed in the things that matter most. Aunts and uncles and cousins would gather around the fire in the winter, and on the porch in the summer, for occasions of no particular purpose other than to be together. From these family stories heard in my childhood, I learned the values of my family, what was expected of us, and who we were. I learned who *I* was in this family. We were the Johnsons, and each person had a life to share that showed how we were to conduct ourselves before God and before our fellow man.

I also was in a family of Doughtys. They held the same values as the Johnsons. They worshipped the same Jesus and drew together in times when tragedy struck in big ways. I watched them manage grief, with confidence in their God, always moving toward God and not away from Him—no matter what. Many simple and memorable times were had by my cousins and me at the home of our grandparents, in their expansive yard, and especially in the branches of their many climbing trees. I think we took for granted the stability of those early times, and the constancy of the faith of our parents and of our aunts and uncles.

Since then, the world has become a very different place, a place where stability is hard to come by. But there is a memory in all of us, the vision of a path to follow. Our early families lived and died by the tenets of the Bible, and though the times are very different now, God remains the Constant—the God of our fathers, the God of us, and the God of our children and grandchildren.

It would certainly be amiss to say that our family was without problems, without flaws, conflicts, and tragedies. We were no exception to the human dilemma. So, to all the mixed-up, messed-up, dysfunctional situations that plague our daily lives, I just say that the solution to each of these problems is the same as it has always been: *Know God better.*

These stories have been gathered not only from family, but also from friends, and even strangers. These stories illustrate the truth of God's mercy to a sinful world, and His mercy to each of us sinners in particular. They are sent forth with a prayer that the reader will be encouraged to pay close attention to his or her own stories, and perhaps to find some means of sharing them with others. All of us have many stories to tell in this journey of life, and those of us who have come to know Jesus Christ in a personal and saving way have, in our stories, incredible accounts of the way our Creator has interacted with us, urging us always to know Him better, to go deeper. And for those who do not yet know Him in a personal relationship, His footprints are in their lives as well—always following, always beckoning to come closer.

All the stories are true, but the names have been changed to protect privacy. And those stories written in the first person are not necessarily my or my family's personal stories, but just written from the perspective of the one who told the story to me.

Georgette, Where Are You?

*I*t was the summer of my fifteenth year, and I was consumed with misery. My family was moving from my native state of Alabama to the state of Florida. I had seldom even *visited* out of my home state, and the Deep South culture of Alabama was the sum total of my whole experience in life. Furthermore, I was about to begin my senior year in high school (expecting to graduate early), and I would be leaving all my friends and everything familiar to me. In my way of thinking, I might as well have been moving to China.

But we had to go, it seemed, for financial reasons. My mother had become the main breadwinner in the home because of my father's poor health, and as a schoolteacher, she received a substantial raise in pay by moving.

The added advantage, and the only one I really liked, was the fact that my brother and sister-in-law lived in Orlando, the city in Florida that we were moving to. But even that did not seem to compensate for the very practical matter in my mind that I would be leaving friends of a lifetime and spending my senior year of high school with total strangers. I couldn't seem to adjust to the idea, although I had some vague idea that God would help me get through this—especially since I had just recently struck up a bargain with Him. I had told Him that my simple request was to live a peaceful and anxiety-free life—in exchange for which I would serve Him my whole life. In my immature mind, I thought God was getting a good deal in the exchange. In His mercy,

God did not choose to teach me swiftly and terribly that I held no bargaining chips with which to negotiate.

We arrived in Florida in early August, before school was starting in September. We moved into a small duplex, where we stayed to await the building of a modest house. We were so cramped for space that, as my father said, "When the cat comes in, we are overdone." Other issues of adjustment included the searing heat (which somehow felt different from Alabama heat) and the extreme difference in the way the whole environment looked. The houses were different, the plants were different, and the people were different. For me, all these things created an upsetting combination. I couldn't seem to find any familiar ground. My southern accent tended to draw a lot of attention among people who wanted to hear additional syllables added to every word, so I became increasingly reluctant to open my mouth in public. Finally, my *attitude* that my life was in ruins was the ultimate guarantee that I would continue in my misery. I was a true victim in my own mind. I thought I had gotten about as low as I could get, but the Lord was about to serve me with a very valuable lesson—and things would get worse before they got better.

Sometime between our arrival in Florida and the beginning of school, my parents, as they were doing errands one day, spotted an elderly woman who was clearly struggling to keep moving. She was a large-framed woman with wild-looking white hair and a bent form not uncommon to her age. They found her walking along the hot streets of our neighborhood, red faced, pouring sweat, and looking as if she would soon die from the heat. She was carrying a single brown paper bag, which turned out to be the sum total of her worldly goods. Mother and Daddy saw the seriousness of her plight against the elements, and they stopped to offer her a ride to wherever she was going. Thus began an association that added enormously to the stress of the next several months.

As it turned out, Georgette, as this large and loud woman was called, did not actually *have* a home. Neither did she claim to have any relatives, friends, or even acquaintances. She was simply *here now*—and very needy. My parents had a long history of compassion for the poor, and they took this dilemma as something that required their help to solve. Indeed, this felt very much like an assignment from the Lord, in spite of their own chaotic lives. So, the offer of a ride turned into a need for a place for her to live. In the course of that same day, they managed to locate a small room for rent that was near our own duplex. I don't recall the arrangements, but they more than likely paid her rent, and they saw to it that she was set up in a decent place to live and was no longer homeless. They searched for other provisions to meet her basic needs (which seemed enormous and very time consuming). We all began to absorb an extra life into our new world.

Georgette became to me the perfect model of obnoxiousness and undesirability. She was a person whose personal hygiene was seriously amiss, and whose speech was loud, opinionated, and provocative. She blasted out words in such a harsh nasal tone, and with an accent so foreign to me, that I thought at times I could not tolerate another word from her. She sounded to me more like a foghorn than a person. And I might add that none of these traits ever changed for the duration of our association with her. She remained totally immune to the heroic efforts of my parents to teach her that, at the very least, daily baths and use of deodorant were a great asset in this culture. But she was who she was, and nothing was to be done about it.

These efforts to rehabilitate Georgette ultimately did not seem important to Mother and Daddy, since they believed that the Lord had put her in our pathway and she needed our help no matter what. Nothing could shake them from this position. We had always befriended people, and doing so came very naturally, but we never had anyone require of us what Georgette required. She happily attached herself to us and showed up daily to see what we would all be doing together. She participated with us as if she were our grandmother or some other close relative in our family. She loved to go on errands with us, she loved to just sit and talk with us, and she loved to watch TV with us. Whatever we did,

Georgette loved to do it with us. And although it was certainly a trial to my parents at times, they knew she was lonely and apparently without a family. In fact, you could get the impression that she *never* had a family, as there was no talk about her past or anyone in it. The present was what she was about. She talked loudly, sharply, and endlessly, and she freely gave her opinion and advice in every matter.

As for me, I knew at some deep level that my parents were right to care for Georgette, but being caught up in my own self-absorption, the stress of being around her just about finished me off. My life, in fact, seemed to be in shambles, worse than I could ever remember, and I routinely thought I could not bear another moment of this shrieking, smelly, bossy old woman. Fortunately, I had enough compassion (or fear of my parents) to not treat her rudely, but I'm sure I got no credit from the Lord because of the attitude of my heart. And I complained aloud to my parents when Georgette was not present (those rare times).

My frustration came to a head the day Mother dropped me off at the high school to register for classes that fall. It was a very depressing job for me to face the reality of this new school. And the crowning blow was when I was informed that I would not get to follow the plans I had long held to take certain specific courses my senior year. It seemed that there were requirements in this new school that were quite different from those of my former school. Home economics, for example, was required of all girls. That had to take the place of French 3, which I had always planned to take. There were other snags, and my final schedule was very upsetting to me. I could not get around these new requirements, so I signed on, trying to hold back the tears until I could get safely back in the car with Mother. I couldn't wait to tell her how messed up my whole life was. I rushed out, spotted our car, and bolted toward it. Then I suddenly saw a familiar form sitting boldly in the front seat with Mother—Georgette! And she was talking so loudly that I could hear her well before I got to the car. I was furious! It was like the last offense I could possibly tolerate. I wanted to scream. I wanted to order her right out of the car and tell her to go drive some other family crazy. The only thing that kept me from saying scorching, ugly things was the absolute certainty that my mother would *not* put up with such an outburst—not for one minute. So, I just got in the backseat and kept my mouth shut until I felt I would not start crying if I spoke. When I did finally manage to try to tell Mother about my disappointment, Georgette pelted me with unsolicited advice, and I ended up even more furious.

Soon after this incident, we had a family discussion about the problem of Georgette. I was generally upset with everything, but Georgette was the specific target on whom I was focusing. Mother and Daddy and I rehearsed the situation as we had done before, and my parents stated again their commitment to befriend Georgette. My father admitted that he was also often weary of her presence, and we all agreed on the challenges involved in this situation. But this was not to be about our inconvenience and what we liked or did not like. It always returned to the question of what was the *right* thing to do. My parents called me to a higher standard than to think only about myself. As always, my father urged me to try to walk in someone else's shoes. He asked if I would like to face Georgette and tell her that she should not come back. Since the biblical mandate to reach out to the poor was clear, he said, we would be given the grace to follow it.

The thought of me personally asking Georgette to leave jolted my thinking. It made me realize I could not face myself if I were so unkind. And I knew that I needed to ask God to help me with my attitude. I knew I was a mess, and I sadly admitted that my peace was gone—that which I thought was assured to me from my earlier "bargain" with God. I knew it was my attitude that had cost me my peace. I knew I had a very bad attitude toward a lot more than Georgette.

I was humbled by realizing the hardness of my heart and my overall selfishness. I began to ask God for help with all my issues. I started reading scripture seriously and consistently for the first time in my life. It did not happen suddenly, but the Lord began to give me the grace to regard Georgette in a new light. I was still irritated at times (as we all were), but, eventually, I began to accept her as a part of our family. My relationship with her began to blossom, as I would often kid around with her and listen to her opinions with a genuine interest. I did not take her blunt comments personally anymore. There were times when I truly was glad to see her hobble up to our door. Sometimes I gave her enthusiastic hugs, and she was obviously pleased, as she tried in her own way to return affection.

Sometimes the cultural contrast between the three of us and Georgette would strike me as hilarious. We would sit three abreast on the couch—Mother, Georgette, and I—with Daddy looking on from his recliner. Georgette had a somewhat wild look, with her white, uncombed curls and her ruddy face, all of which seemed to match her speech. My parents and I all drawled out our words at a snail's pace, using round, warm sounds. In contrast to our speaking style, Georgette's words flew past us at the speed of a rocket—and, with its nasal tone, her voice sounded to us like someone scratching a blackboard. Her volume was about twice that of ours, and I can remember my father wincing at times as she blasted out her words all over our little place, shattering the peace. I would occasionally laugh out loud at the group we made. Daddy and I would wink at each other in secret fun, amused at the differences between us and the woman we had befriended.

We spoke to Georgette about the Lord, and she listened, not disagreeing or showing disrespect. She nodded quietly, as if the name of God should not be shouted about. She believed in God.

We knew Georgette loved us, and she knew we all loved her. Even I had come to love her, and she seemed to know that too. At last, I was able to look past the surface issues to see the lonely old lady God had sent into our lives. We had fallen into a routine with her. She ate dinner with us every night, and she spent the evenings doing whatever we were doing. It seemed as if she had always been with us and always would be.

But after several months of coexisting with Georgette, quite a startling thing happened. In a casual conversation one day, she announced that she would need to leave us soon. She looked lovingly at us, but not sadly, not as if she were expecting a disaster. To this comment, she would add no more information, but then she continued to show up for our daily fellowship as usual. We had no idea what she meant and soon we forgot about the comment.

Then one day, she simply did not show up at our house. We were immediately alarmed and went looking for her. Her little rented room was left untouched. The landlady had no idea of her whereabouts. We began a serious search for her, fearing that she had been hit by a car or taken ill somewhere. We did not find her that day or in the days that followed. We routinely drove up and down all the streets in the area—any distance she could have possibly walked—and she simply was not there. We called hospitals and police. There were no clues, no trace of her having lived or died—except for the sparse things in her room. We looked over her room again. Nothing was missing except Georgette. All her things, her few clothes and even her old brown paper bag, were left behind. We were completely baffled—and very sad. We kept looking, not knowing what else to do, and every evening when she did not show up at our door for dinner and an evening with us, we grew sadder. We each had a time of crying out of concern for her—and really missing her. She had truly become a part of our family.

One afternoon after school, I was sitting on my bed reading my Bible and still wondering about Georgette. On this particular day, I read a verse in Hebrews that got my undivided attention: "Do not neglect to show hospitality to strangers, for thereby some have entertained angels unawares" (Hebrews 13:2).

I bolted out of my room to tell Mother and Daddy what I had just read. We looked at one another with amazement as the possibility of this struck us. Daddy said that, of course, we would likely never know the real story of Georgette in this life, but that God had His own purpose for our encounter with her, whether or not she was an angel. We knew we had all been changed for the better.

The move to Florida proved to be a life-changing event for me, a time when I grew in the Lord more than ever before in my life. I began to see that God is at work in every circumstance, especially the really hard ones, such as the Georgette challenge had been to me. I could see clearly that sin was the root of losing one's peace of mind, and I realized that my quest for peace was linked to my willingness to obey. And in all the years that were to come, I would find it much easier to love people who are different. The lesson was a gift from God.

Later, encouraged by the leaders of my church, I was able to tell the story of Georgette in a speakers' tournament sponsored by a number of churches in Florida. Through this experience, I learned to speak comfortably to hundreds of people—in congregations all over the state. I was able to admit my selfish attitude and share what God had taught me through Georgette. And each time I spoke, I felt sad as I recounted the unusual end of the story.

The invaluable lesson I learned from my experience with Georgette has been revisited countless times in my life when I have encountered obnoxious, unlovable people—people easily rejected by others. Many of those people became friends of mine, and, just as in the case of Georgette, in the end, I was greatly blessed by their friendship. I would find that, ultimately, it was hard to remember why I did not like them initially. It was never again as difficult for me to love the unlovable, having won that victory with Georgette.

I have never forgotten the dear old bag lady, and I am confident that I will indeed see her again and learn the end of her story. I don't know if I will meet her as just another saved sinner like myself or as one of God's holy angels sent to help my family grow. But I must remember to thank her. I didn't get a chance to before she left.

Sing a New Song

Oh sing to the Lord a new song,
for He has done marvelous things!
His right hand and His holy arm
have worked salvation for him.

(Psalm 98:1)

Today is the day to remember our wonderful God,
to sing a new song to Him—
a song of renewal,
a song of praise,
a song of thanksgiving.

Today is the day to ask of Him,
"What shall I do to serve you?"
Today is the day to look and see,
and to do what is needed—
joyfully,
praising Him for the privilege,
trusting Him for the gifts given to serve Him,
asking for a will bent to His.

It is no mystery what we are to do;
it is daily revealed:
For today is about the attitude of the heart toward Him,
since from the heart flows the worship that binds us to Him;
since from the heart comes the only service that matters;
so we worship and serve—
from the heart.

And whether we stand on our feet or must sit due to infirmity;
    whether we must lie because we cannot sit,
        and for as long as He gives us our minds,
            or even when our minds are not fully there—
Let us praise Him, let us serve Him
    with all that we have left.
Let us praise Him, let us serve Him
    with our last breath here,
        and our first breath in His Presence.

No, Not Forever ...

*Y*esterday, one of Your saints encouraged me, Lord, although he had no idea of it. In fact, I did not know him, nor did he know me. But I saw his face, and I knew he belonged to You. Actually, I was encouraged by several of Your people, but one injured old saint in particular was the focus of a conversation I overheard.

My husband and I sat in a booth at a restaurant, waiting for our lunch to be served. An elderly couple walked slowly past, and I glanced at them. That's when I knew they were Yours, because I saw the light in their faces. Just in that one glimpse was revealed the peaceful demeanor, the clear, smiling eyes, the hope, the joy. They moved slowly, he with obvious deformity of his shoulder. It was painfully frozen in an awkward position. Still, he had the look of contentment.

They barely passed our table when they were hailed by friends in the booth behind us. They stopped to talk to their friends. After exchanging pleasantries, one friend inquired about the shoulder.

"The shoulder's still a problem?"

"Yes. Nothing can be done about it."

"So, this is it ... forever?"

"Oh, no! Not forever. Just until I get Home. I'll get a new shoulder in heaven!"

All chimed in with happy agreement. Smiles, lilted voices, good cheer among the group, all expecting the same fate. They spoke of You and Your kingdom joyfully.

Later, after a chorus of good-byes, the old couple passed us a second time, their faces speaking even more. They can't wait to see You, Lord, and the frozen shoulder is not an issue—just a temporary inconvenience.

> By faith, Abraham obeyed when he was called to go out to a place that he was to receive as an inheritance. And he went out, not knowing where he was going. By faith, he went to live in the land of promise, as in a foreign land, living in tents with Isaac and Jacob, heirs with him of the same promise. For he was looking forward to the city that has foundations, whose designer and builder is God.
>
> (Hebrews 11:8–10)

> These all died in faith, not having received the things promised, but having seen them and greeted them from afar, and having acknowledged that they were strangers and exiles on the earth. For people who speak thus make it clear that they are seeking a homeland. If they had been thinking of that land from which they had gone out, they would have had opportunity to return. But as it is, they desire a better country, that is, a heavenly one.
>
> Therefore God is not ashamed to be called their God, for he has prepared for them a city. (Hebrews 11:13–15)

This world is not my home I'm just passing through my
treasures are laid up somewhere beyond the blue
the angels beckon me from heaven's open door
and I can't feel at home in this world anymore

(Words and music by Albert Edward Brumley
October 29, 1905 – November, 15, 1977)

Image Bearers

If I bear Your Image, Lord,
   then I must reflect light—
      and not curse the darkness.

And what is light, I ask earnestly.
Speak, Lord, in Your quiet way:

"It is more than 'not darkness,'
   just as good is more than 'not evil.'
It is the primary condition
   of the Eternal God.

Darkness is the permission of choice,
   and only here for a while.
You have been redeemed from the dark,
   and though you walk through it for a season,
      it can do no harm to you unless you assent.

But *you* can harm the darkness;
you can rip its fabric and shred its intent
   with the gospel of peace.
For you bear My image
   and it is not a small thing.

Go forth with the saints
   whose lampstands remain
      until I come to you—
         or you come to Me."

Jesus Loves Jody

$\mathcal{J}$ody was just a few weeks from this second birthday. He was a little blond boy with beautiful blue eyes and a cheerful demeanor. He already loved books and was always curious about the things around him. He was active enough, but not overly so, not requiring constant concern that he must be watched every moment. He was already a big brother and was gentle in playing with his baby sister. He ate well and slept well and was an easy baby in every respect.

It was in the routine setting of daily life that a most extraordinary thing happened. Company was coming for dinner, and Jody's mother was busy with preparations as the children played, more or less quietly, in an adjoining room. All was pretty much childproof, and nothing would seem dangerous in such a setting. Then came nap time for the children, both of whom were good nappers, often sleeping for two hours or more.

After about two hours, Jody's little sister woke up from the nap. Jody continued to sleep, and his mother didn't find it of much concern at this point. However, after three hours, Jody's mother decided she must wake up her son, lest he be unable to sleep that night. When she went to get him up, she was unable to awaken him. It was clear that something was very wrong. Very quickly, Jody's parents rushed him to the nearest hospital, leaving his little sister with a neighbor.

The ER pediatrician made a quick assessment and asked if Jody had taken any pills or other medicine that might be around the house.

Nothing came to mind, because all medicines were put out of reach. The doctor insisted that the father go home and look around for a possible breech in keeping the medicine safely away from the children. It was on this search that Jody's father found some prescription medicine that had been recently given to him by a doctor. The bottle of pills had clearly been opened and was now empty. Unthinkable! This bottle had been sitting on a mantel, seemingly totally out of reach for any young child. Furthermore, Jody was not typically one to climb on things. But, in fact, a chair sat close to the mantel, and it became obvious that Jody *had climbed* and thereby gotten the pills. There had been twenty-two pills left in this prescription, by Jody's father's estimation, and now there were no pills at all. Jody's father duly reported this worst-possible news to the hospital.

When the physician learned of the type and quantity of the pills, he shook his head. Jody had been hooked up to an IV, and he was still unconscious. He was placed under an oxygen tent, for in those days that was how oxygen was administered, rather than by means of a nose apparatus. The tent had a zipper through which nurses could reach in to adjust his IV and check vital signs.

The doctor then had a reality talk with Jody's parents. He told them that it was too late to pump the stomach, because of the time involved. The pills were clearly disseminated into the child's system, and all he could do was try to flush out the system with the IV. He gave the parents the bad news that Jody would likely not survive the effect of ingesting so many of this particular type of pill. If he did, in fact, survive, the doctor said he would almost certainly suffer severe brain damage. The parents got the impression that it would be a mercy for the Lord to just take Jody, rather than to leave him in the expected vegetative state.

Thus began the longest night that they, or any parents, would ever suffer through. Their son was not expected to live until morning. The father went home to see about the baby sister and to deliver her to a relative until the crisis ended. He then returned to the hospital for the long vigil.

Their church was notified and asked for prayer, and the parents sat in Jody's room, watching the hospital staff and doctors doing all they could do to save their son. They attempted to wake him up by pricking his feet and gently shaking him, but his coma was deep, and it seemed he would just slip away without ever regaining consciousness. The doctor stayed the night to do all that was humanly possible. A sense of sorrow was over the hospital wing as the nurses and doctors gazed at the precious little blond child so likely to lose his life.

Sometime in the early part of the night, a couple from their church showed up to pray over Jody. They were barely known by the parents, but all prayer and support was welcome. Unlike anything the parents had witnessed up to that time, they brought a small vial of oil and asked if they could anoint Jody as is sometimes done in a prayer for healing. Of course, they would not be refused, so they reached inside the oxygen tent and touched a drop of oil to the child's forehead. They then put their hands on his little arms, one on each side, and they prayed. They prayed aloud for his miraculous recovery; then they stood silently and prayed. After a considerable time, they proclaimed something very startling to the beleaguered parents.

"You are not to worry about your son," the man said. "The Lord has shown us that he will be fully recovered by the time the sun comes up." He then took leave, but his wife remained for a while, sitting in a nearby chair and continuing to pray silently.

Jody's parents did not know what to make of this; nor did they believe, in all honesty, that this was true. His mother, who told the story, had experience working in the medical field while in college, and she had seen death and near death. She knew all the signs, and she saw the death pall on her son. She saw the labored breathing, and she knew that he could only last a matter of hours. She was a woman of faith, but she knew that terrible things happen to all of us. As much as she wanted to believe this well-meaning couple, she could not believe her son would recover. She thanked them with many tears, however, and was very grateful to be shown such love at this unbearable time.

The terrible hours of the night then silently crept by—with only the parents sitting watch over their precious child. His mother sat in a chair at the foot of his bed and kept her hand on his little leg. No sign of life was there apart from the labored breathing. The nurses came and went, changing his IV as needed and still trying to wake him up—but without success.

At one point in the early hours of the morning, the nurse removed the IV and was about to replace it with another, but she had to temporarily leave the room, called to some other purpose, and told the mother she would return in a moment to replace the IV.

The mother, exhausted from grief, lay her head down on the bed, still holding her son's leg. She prayed desperately, but really without hope for her son's life. Never did she doubt the goodness of God, but somehow her faith had not been tested in such a crucible as this—to ask for the impossible. She just knew for certain that her Lord would strengthen her to face whatever was required.

Then a dreamlike thing happened. The mother felt the bed move, her son's leg move. She thought she must be falling asleep and in some sort of twilight state. But the leg jerked away from her hand, and the bed moved even more. The mother sat up—just in time to see Jody climbing around the side rails of the bed and scrambling to the floor. He had crawled through the unzipped side of his oxygen tent to escape, and faster than she could fully comprehend what was happening, he was on the floor and heading out the open door. Still thinking it was a mirage, she hesitated a moment, and then jerked herself to full attention to recognize that Jody was out of the room altogether. She suddenly focused on what was happening, whether dream or not, and she jumped up and ran after her son.

In the hallway, she saw his speedy little legs racing away, with the hospital gown flapping open behind him. She sped after him, finding him difficult to catch. A nurse saw what was happening and began to call for the doctor. At once, a team of medical help was in the hall witnessing the spectacular sight. The mother got to him first. They were at the end of the corridor of the hospital wing, where a large window looked out over the city and ushered in the first glorious rays of morning. The mother stooped to take her son into her arms, and as she did, she saw the morning light and remembered what their visitor had said: "You are not to worry about your son. The Lord has shown us that he will be fully recovered by the time the sun comes up."

She could no longer stand up by herself but collapsed on the floor, holding her child. She was weeping uncontrollably. The doctor was soon at the scene, along with at least two nurses. The mother finally stood, and the group of them gathered in embraces, as Jody was being hugged in the middle of the circle they formed. There were no words ...

But, at last, there *were* words—from the doctor. He said to the mother, "You must not completely get your hopes up about the overall results of this. Surely he will live, and this looks incredible, but if there is *no* brain damage, we will have seen our second miracle. We will keep him under observation and do some testing for the next couple of days."

So it was for the next forty-eight hours or so that Jody was under close scrutiny by many hospital personnel. He fell back sleep and into a very normal pattern. He woke up after a few hours of true rest and showed no sign of any effects of the deadly medicine he had taken. Indeed, he sat up in his bed and chatted happily with his mother, playing with the toys and books that had found their way to his side. His mother sat, gazing at him, trying not to weep continually out of gratitude to God, for she knew that a miracle had happened and that it was no thanks to her own faith, but to the faith of virtual strangers—and, of course, entirely owed to the goodness of God who had answered their prayers and even given them a sign of confirmation: "He will be fully recovered by the time the sun comes up …" God had even led Jody to the window to show everyone the sunrise.

And for the grand finish of this story, the next day, as the mother sat quietly looking at her precious child and praising God for His mercy, Jody suddenly looked up from his play, with a big smile, and said simply, "Jesus loves Jody."

Only Once

This Jesus, once infant, but always King;
     born as one of us,
          yet *not* one of us ...

Gifts placed before Him by earthly kings;
Gift of gifts returned to us
     in His young manhood—
          offering life for life—
     His life for ours.

Never a child born like this One—
A light within Himself,
     shining redemption into lost souls.
Offering salt to pour over the tasteless food
     of the world's table.

And calling us to a Feast Unparalleled,
     hosted by the Great King,
          once laid in a manger
          amid the beasts.

Holy Ground

A lovely young woman stepped up to the podium at a church we were visiting in Vermont several years ago. She had been asked to sing a beautiful, poignant song of worship—and, indeed, that is what she did. Her voice was like an angel's offering up to God. But it was not the song that created the memory to last over these years. It was the story she told us before she sang.

She was going to sing a favorite song of her grandfather, the man who had raised her, along with an aunt. These two, she told us, were true followers of Christ—imparting to her the witness of a deep and abiding faith. *It was a faith that held firm in life and in death.*

Her grandfather spoke of Jesus as One ever present with him, One who was revered, loved, and trusted completely. He taught the young woman the riches of the scripture, the source by which he lived daily. Because of him, she knew from early on the great stories of the Bible, the great truths, the great recording of God's interaction with His people.

One of the stories about God's servant, Moses, was to be imprinted on her mind forever. It was the time when God called Moses out of his quiet, desert-dwelling life of forty years and gave him the assignment that would alter all of history. The assignment was to return to Egypt and lead his people out of captivity—to reshape them as a nation and lead them back home to the land God had promised Abraham many hundreds of years earlier.

To get his attention, God spoke to Moses through a burning bush that would not be consumed by the flames. As Moses drew near to this astonishing sight, God spoke to him from the bush. God first let Moses know that this was not some sleight-of-hand trick. It was the Great and Only God who spoke directly to Moses that day: "Do not come near; take your sandals off your feet, for the place on which you are standing is holy ground" (Exodus 3:5).

Moses heard the voice of the sovereign Lord; he felt the Holy Presence; he felt his own unworthiness. He hid his face because he was afraid.

This story, the young woman told us, held a special place in her heart, for it was connected to the end of her grandfather's time on earth. As he climbed the stairs of his home one day in his old age, it was the day that God had marked for his homecoming to heaven. When he reached the top of the stairs, he clutched his heart and fell to the floor. His daughter, the young woman's aunt, heard him fall and rushed to his side.

The old man recognized this to be his call Home. Even in his pain, he was elated. His last victorious words were to his daughter: "Take off my shoes, Daughter, for I'm standing on holy ground!"

She did as he asked. Then he, like Moses, was in the Presence of the Living God. But unlike Moses, he could come very close. The cross of Jesus had made him worthy.

Her grandfather's faith held firm in life and in death.

In His Presence

In His Presence ...
What to do
    when the Power presses in—
      Raise hands in praise?
      Bow head in reverence?
      Dance with joy?
      Shout with glee?

All these are worship,
  but not enough.

Face on the ground,
  arms spread out,
  drained of self,
  prostrate before the great I Am.

Pressed down to nothing.
Lifted up to glorious joy ...
  in His Presence.

Sears Roebuck Catalog as Moral Guide

$\mathscr{A}$lmost every American can recognize the name *Sears*. We know the store, we know what it sells, and we know it as part of Americana. But you have to be a certain age to be able to identify the *Roebuck* part. And when I was growing up, Sears always went with Roebuck.

So, what was so great about Sears Roebuck and Company? I can tell you with all certainty that, in our household, it was their catalog. For one thing, it was *free* in those days. It came to your door seasonally and quickly became the family dream book. Every member of the family was interested in its contents and pored over its pages from cover to cover, especially those of us who lived in small towns, accustomed to "basics only" in our shopping possibilities. For us, the Sears Roebuck catalog was a spellbinding look at the most incredible goods, and without that catalog, we hardly would have known such items even existed.

Every member of our family had his or her special-interest section. Daddy loved Sears Roebuck tools and equipment. My older brother longingly dreamed over the sports equipment, and my mother lingered over the curtains and bedspreads and the women's clothing. As for me, I was very young, but even so, I had a slight interest in the clothes on all the little girls in the catalog and a really *big* interest in the toys. And so we dreamed through the pages, circling our favorites, checking our wishes, and all the while knowing that we could not possibly buy much at all.

Now it is the above scenario that was no doubt the intent of dear Mr. Sears and Mr. Roebuck when they furnished us our dream book. We were supposed to look and be wowed, figure what could be had, and then, of course, we were supposed to *order*. In this, we fulfilled our duty. But in the spirit of maximizing a good thing, we also had other plans for our catalog. We could tear out the pages to help start a fire in the fireplace, for example. But before this happened, and after the initial longings were satisfied by everyone in the family, I would finally get a chance to monopolize the marvelous treasure; my personal favorite use of the catalog would then be possible.

I would watch diligently for my father to sit down in his rocking chair by the fire in the evening after supper. Just as he barely landed in his chair, and before he could take up some other diversion, I would appear at his feet, armed with the catalog. This was a two-arms-full task for me, and I cradled the catalog tentatively, puffing with effort, just long enough to get Daddy to pick up both me and the catalog and place us in the proper spot on his lap. Then I would release my treasured book to him, and he would feign ignorance of my plan.

"Why are you toting around this big book, little girl?" he would inquire.

And I would inform him anew each time that I wanted him to tell me a story from this book, to which he would say, "Why, this is the Sears Roebuck catalog. What makes you think there is a story in this?"

I would play out my role, assuring him that there were *many* stories in this great book and that he knew all of them! And he would act as if he was surprised and doubtful that this was true. But he would nevertheless open up the book, cautiously looking at me, as if I were surely wrong; but he would at least check it out. Then he would thumb through the pages casually, and, eventually, he would just "happen upon" the section of sketch drawings of children (wearing Sears Roebuck children's clothing, of course). They would be standing in various poses, sometimes seeming to interact with one another, but, overall, looking pretty bland. At this point, I would get a rush of excitement because I knew there was nothing boring, bland, or common about this section of the catalog. No, indeed, for I had already been trained in the school of Daddy's imagination, and I knew for sure that high adventure was on the way, as these characters would spring to life and make known their various plights.

Daddy would gaze at the pictures as if he were hearing them speak to him. He would listen with amazed expression to their stories, glancing at me to let me know I was going to be astonished when he shared what he heard. At last, he would turn to me with a magical twinkle in his eyes.

"Oh yes, Charlotte Ann, you were right! Just wait until you hear what is happening to Mary Margaret and Linda Lou!" (Virtually everyone had a double name in the South in those days).

And we were off and running. Every child in these illustrations had a name and a story to tell. They often knew one another, and their stories intertwined in endless, creative ways. There were disputes, there were triumphs, there were dangers, and there were invisible fairies and fairy-tale characters who inserted themselves into the mix of the visible drawings. There was a veritable treasure trove of places and landscapes and descriptions that surrounded these little dress models. Bland? Oh no, indeed! The catalog was a living landscape of imaginings, clearly painted with Daddy's enthusiastic words. How grand it was to be cradled in his left arm, while his right arm was free to gesture and add to the animation of our catalog journey. Life was good!

There were conversations between the children—and oh, what conversations! Some sassy little girl might say something sharp that hurt the feelings of the girl to her right. Oh, how terrible that was to Daddy and me! We couldn't understand why someone would be so unkind. We would feel awful for the poor victim of the sharp tongue. We would say to each other how we would feel if someone said that to us. Alas and alack! Could things be brought aright? Oh yes, they could! The offending child would likely have an attack of conscience and then apologize. The offended child would forgive her, and they would be friends. Or perhaps the guilty party would have to learn a thing or two herself after someone down the line of drawings came forth and treated *her* badly. *Then* she got the picture and she realized how it felt to be treated in such a manner. And, of course, she repented and made amends. But sometimes these things did not work out so well right away. Some villainous children would dig in their heels and refuse to do the right thing. We might have to leave them in such a frightful state until tomorrow night—or even longer. Oh, that was unsettling! An unrepentant villain on the loose in the catalog—very unnerving. I would think about this as I fell asleep that night and hope against hope that other children would not also be wounded before Daddy could fix things among them. But some circumstance in this catalog of life would eventually show the consequences of such behavior, and the foolish children would come to their senses.

Wonderful stories jumped off the pages of Sears Roebuck catalog, night after night. I knew all the names of the children. I knew their stories as well as those of the *unseen* cast of characters that was also very much a part of the children's stories. And always, Daddy opened up the hearts of these little models and let me see how fragile they were, even those who were acting out. He showed me the healing power of kindness and forgiveness, and the devastation of selfishness and anger. I gained a world-class education by walking in the shoes of others. I learned how to share, to return good for evil, to forgive, and to be a friend. And I learned that God was very pleased when my heart was set on goodness.

And so the names of Mr. Sears and Mr. Roebuck sounded magical to me. I liked their catalog. And I liked their store. On the rare occasions that we journeyed to a town large enough to have one of their stores, I was excited to step inside and get a glimpse of some of the very wonderful things that I had only known as pictures.

But where are the children? I wondered, the first time I remember us going to the real store. I looked for them behind the appliances, among the tools, and even peeking around the cash registers where the clerks lived. Daddy was able to clear up the mystery. The children, he said, had to remain in the catalog. After all, if they showed up at a store, then only the people in *that* store could meet them, and all the other children everywhere would be disappointed. The catalog was where they lived so that they could be shared by all who visited those pages. And, oh yes, they had mothers and daddies just like me. All my concerns were laid to rest.

Now who shall I thank for these experiences, foundational to the rest of my life? Shall I thank the wonderful store and the catalog that reached out to us in rural America? Yes, I do give thanks, and I have always had a special place in my heart for Sears Roebuck (I still think of the original name). Shall I thank the father who forfeited his newspaper and whatever else he might have enjoyed doing during his very limited time of rest—who, instead, made a loving investment in his young daughter, who used his considerable creativity and the strength of his beliefs to teach lessons that would never be forgotten? Oh yes, I do so thank my father! He was a rock in my life. But, most importantly, I saw that my rock had another Rock. I heard him speak about the Rock of the Son of God. I saw clearly that this Rock was behind all the reasons for our every decision, our every action. The Rock was the standard against which we measured everything. And, surely, He loved us with an everlasting love.

Thank you, Daddy, for making it so easy to love God. You gave *Father* the best-possible name. And thank You, God, for giving me such a father. It is *You* to whom I am most indebted.

Small Gifts

O Lord, let me gather the treasures here
    which I can bring with me
        and lay at Your feet—

        gifts of love,
        gifts of service,
        gifts of praise,
        gifts of thanksgiving—

Not because I can earn Your favor,
    or repay the debt for my soul;

But just hoping to offer to You
    the joy of a Parent who is blessed
        by a grateful child's small offerings of love.

In the Employment of the Lord

*R*achael was a home-care nurse in South Florida. Her job had taken on a whole new meaning since she had become a Christian, for she knew that everything she did was "as unto the Lord." She was daily filled with the joy of the Lord and was eager for any opportunity to share her faith.

There was an occasion when Rachael was directed to visit a new patient, one who was not actually in her travel area. This case was assigned to her because the person who would normally have signed up this new case was not available to do so at that time. Of course, those who are serving the Lord know that there are no accidents or coincidences in God's directing of their lives, that everything has a purpose, even when it may never be known in this life. She proceeded to carry out this new assignment.

Rachael arrived at the complex where the new patient lived. It looked very nice on the outside, but when she was admitted entrance by the daughter of the patient, the inside was a different story. She immediately saw the patient sitting in very uncomfortable and inconvenient surroundings, and obviously very short of breath due to her emphysema. The daughter seemed rather unconcerned, and there were also a number of creepy-looking men skulking around the place. The windows on the inside were dirty, and the overall impression was very depressing.

Rachael examined the woman and began to comfort her in her illness. She announced to the daughter and the others present that the patient needed to be in better circumstances. She needed to be placed in a clean area which was set up conveniently for the woman to get around. In a professional manner, Rachael explained all that was needed, and her words carried a certain authority. She said she would return the next day to inspect the situation again.

But, before leaving, Rachael got an assignment from the Lord, and the assignment was to have prayer with those who were present. She asked the daughter for permission to pray for her mother. The daughter was embarrassed and probably shamed over the whole situation, so she reluctantly agreed. Rachael then proceeded to ask God's blessing on the patient and the household. She then left, again with a promise to return the following day.

The next day, Rachael did return to see her new patient. She was pleasantly surprised to find that the very ill woman had been set up in a top-floor room overlooking the water, a beautiful setting. The windows were clean, and the room was conveniently arranged. Rachael was very pleased with this new arrangement, and she began to talk to her patient about her circumstances. But the physical conditions were not even the most serious of the woman's issues.

As she and Rachael talked, the woman confided in Rachael that she believed her daughter was eager for her to die so that she could claim the condominium for herself. It was certainly a tragic story. Rachael knew that she needed to speak to the woman about the only thing that really mattered. She told her that what really counted was not these sad circumstances. She asked her if she had ever asked Jesus to save her and to assure her of a relationship with Him. The woman did not know what she meant, and Rachael explained what was needed. The woman looked very hopeful and said she would like to invite the Lord to be her Savior. They prayed together, and the woman was astonished as she felt the Presence and power of the Lord in the room. The sun shone brilliantly through the window, adding the physical beauty to the miracle of a rescued soul. The two women shared this remarkable moment of transformation and hope. Rachael left the place, filled with joy to see the woman filled with hope and peace. She told the patient she would return to see her soon.

Rachael decided to call her manager and request that the new client be assigned to her, even though she was not in her territory. With this now-strong bond between them, Rachael wanted to continue to minister to this newly born child of God. The next day, she called to make this request. She was shocked when told that the woman had died the previous day.

This is indeed a story of victory. It is a story of God's timing and God's intent to save. The Lord had in mind to give a sick and beleaguered woman a chance to stand healed in His Presence, both in body and spirit. He sent His servant, Rachael, who listened to His Voice and obeyed Him. He gave her a boldness and a clear mission, and the power of the Holy Spirit did the work of salvation. It was a very brief encounter between two women; however, Rachael has a blazing memory of the beauty of all that happened, and she has a new friend in heaven waiting to thank her. And she has all of eternity to get better acquainted with her new sister in Christ.

Joy as Truth

Joy is the normal fare of heaven.
Joy is different from happiness.
Joy is even a step above contentment—
    but it can't happen without it.

Joy flows directly out of thankfulness;
    Therefore, it is not dependent
        on circumstances—good or bad.
Its foundation is trust in absolute Truth.

Jesus said, "I am ... the truth ..." (John 15:6)
Trust in the Truth of Jesus,
    that He has all things covered,
    that He will win, has won, and has never lost *anything.*

I am with Him;
I am covered.
I will see Him face-to-face.
I will taste of heaven while I am here—
    when I take hold, *really take hold,* of Truth;
    when I am filled with thankfulness in all things.

The Friend Joy will sweep me up
    to give a glimpse of eternity.
I can keep joy for as long as I bow down
    and give thanks—even here.

Too Late, Mr. D.

My cousin and I were having a rare day that we could spend together, and, as always, thoroughly enjoying reminding each other of our family stories, especially the ones of those we loved who had long since passed on to eternity. We had traveled back to the very small town where we both had early beginnings, and, eventually, we made our way to the little cemetery on the edge of town. Remote and beautifully set against the woods, it was reached by an unpaved country road. It was a silent place, a place of deep peace to both of us because we had returned there so many times. We had returned to bury our people, one by one; we had returned to stand with friends in their losses; and we had returned, as on this particular day, just to visit and remember.

We looked at the names of our grandparents, our aunts, our uncles, our cousins—some names so removed from us in time that we had never known them, but only knew *of* them from stories we had heard. We wandered over the familiar plots of friends and families, and recalled much.

We paused over a particular grave. It was conspicuous because of the uniquely elaborate headstone standing among more common stones— signifying not only a difference in death but also in life. Yes, we knew this name well. Our uncle had worked for him back when the man was the owner of the only general merchandise store in our little town. My father, once an official of our town, had known him well in the context of sharing in local leadership and conducting the business of the town.

This merchant—I'll call him Mr. D.—whose grave we stood above, had kept us all supplied with basic needs, had drawn in horses and wagons from the farmlands in those days of our childhood, and had supplied the rural farmers—as well as all of us townspeople—with dry goods of every sort. He was known far and wide in those parts and had been a benefit to all our lives. My cousin and I were silent for a time. We recognized this man's important role to our childhood community. But there was more to be said. Yes, another memory of him would surface at the mere sight of his name. We didn't want it to surface, but there it was. In fact, it was the *first* memory of him.

"So sad," my cousin said.

I agreed.

My husband needed an explanation. So it came out—the long-standing knowledge of a man's reputation. The fact was that his love of money had pushed integrity to the side. Mr. D. was a very wealthy man—something to be applauded as the American dream, something no one held against him. The problem was that the way in which he made a lot of that money caused harm to others. He squeezed the employees for their pennies, taking back as much of their poor means as he could creatively manage to do by various forms of chicanery. The customers, while dependent on his store to provide basic needs, were wary of the many ways he could seem to cut them short. Over the years, the general consensus was that this man would stop at nothing to gain his next dime. His fellow citizens needed his merchandise, but they had to watch their backs at all times.

This wealthy man also acquired a great deal of property, on much of which he held mortgages. Debts were suddenly called in by unscrupulous tricks levied against uneducated people, and very conveniently, Mr. D. waited in the wings, with open arms to catch the poor shacks of these unfortunate ones. It was quite a house-acquisition plan. Mr. D. then would rent his acquired property, often back to the very farmer who had lost it—but beware of *that* arrangement! There was a good chance that the rental house would mysteriously burn to the ground, and a nice insurance settlement would be awarded to Mr. D.—for he was always heavily insured, and he was always glad to get rid of his shacks and get paid to do it. It was well said of those who lived in this man's houses that they had better "sleep with one eye open."

So here we stood, my cousin and me, still alive to tell the story at least forty years after Mr. D's death. It was his greed and dishonesty that we remembered most about him. Yes, his gravestone was better than the rest in the cemetery, and he certainly had died with far more money than anyone else lying in that graveyard. But what he did not have—and could never redeem—was his good name.

It is too late, Mr. D. And how do you see this now, from your new vantage point? But yet, I thank you, for you have spoken to me from your grave and made me ask what will be said of me by those who stand over *my* grave. Only by the grace of God will I fare any better.

A good name is to be chosen rather than great riches. (Proverbs 22:1)

The Lord Was Her Shepherd

*M*s. Muriel became an early friend when we were newcomers to the church where she attended. She was an elderly saint who swept everyone into her circle of love and kindness. It was obvious that she had a lot of pain, often wearing a neck brace and carrying a cushion so that she could sit through various church activities, but this she bore with equanimity, always thanking God that she was doing as well as she was. She loved to talk about her former work with children and young people, and said many times how much she regretted having to give up her ministry to them because of her physical limitations. She said these things not as a complaint, but as a longing to serve God in a greater way, as she had in the past.

We were not there to see Ms. Muriel's early service to the Lord, but we did see clearly her ministry in her last years, for we, and virtually everyone else, were recipients of it. She could hardly have served more at any age. She knew who was sick and who had trouble in the church body, and she was a constant visitor to those in need. She was a card sender second to none. As long as she was able, she would fix little lunches and invite people to her house for a time of fellowship. She would likely give a cutting of a flower to anyone who came, for she was also a lover of plants. She painted cheery pictures which were displayed in her home—or given away to others. She might offer you some treasure from her home if you visited her.

So much more could be said, for the list of her kindnesses seemed endless, but, above all, the thing which should be said was that Ms. Muriel loved

Jesus. It was her great desire that all should know Him, should trust in Him for eternal salvation, and should serve Him faithfully in this life. This was indeed what she did herself; it was the standard by which she lived and died, and she clearly blazed a trail for others to follow.

During her last days on earth, Ms. Muriel had many challenges with surgery, infections, and pain, but she was blessed to have a peaceful place to stay at the end, surrounded by family and friends. She was ultimately able to be free of pain and allowed to just begin the journey to see her Lord without further ado. So many people remembered when she had reached out to them, and they came to repay her in some small way, to encourage her, and to rejoice with her about her glorious future. Joy, not sorrow, was the feeling of those who were also redeemed by the cross of Christ, and knew with certainty that this parting would be temporary.

Some friends had visited Ms. Muriel the week before she went to heaven. She was unable to speak, and her eyes were closed; nevertheless, they spoke to her, believing she could hear them. They read scripture and sang and prayed—and determined that they would visit again soon if God had not taken her Home. They returned the following week and were amazed to see her with her eyes open and seeming to understand her surroundings much better than the week before. One of the three had arrived ahead of the other two and began to sing to her and read scripture. An older woman came into the peaceful room during this time, a volunteer at the hospice, and she joined in with the joyful praise, for she too was a follower of Christ, so the bond was instant among the three of them. As the friend began to read the Twenty-Third Psalm to Ms. Muriel, the volunteer said, "Look! She is saying the words with you!" And it was true. Though she could not speak, her mouth formed the words of the Psalm:

"The Lord is my Shepherd; I shall not want ..." (Psalm 23:1).

Through each line, she followed with her lips ...

"Even though I walk through the valley of the shadow of death, I will fear no evil …" (Psalm 23:4).

On she went, silently forming the immortal words …

"And I shall dwell in the house of the Lord forever" (Psalm 23:6).

The other two friends arrived, and the joyful fellowship continued. They read the scripture, they prayed, and they sang—and they talked of the marvelous days ahead for Ms. Muriel and all the saints of God.

Some of Ms. Muriel's relatives arrived, and the friends wanted to respectfully leave so that the family could be with their dear one. As a last good-bye, they sang "I Have Decided to Follow Jesus." They kissed their friend good-bye, and one said, "You have done the most important thing, Ms. Muriel, and now your reward comes."

They all felt that this would be the last time in this life to see their friend, for God often gives a rally of sorts before life ends. They had seen the rally, they had worshipped with her, and they were rejoicing for her, even with a little longing themselves—for she was about to see Jesus face-to-face.

Only a few hours later, as the Wednesday night fellowship began at Ms. Muriel's church, the announcement came to the group: Ms. Muriel was Home at last! A murmur of sorrow and joy went up among them. They would miss her so very much, but oh how they praised God, and they tried to imagine the extent of her joy at that moment!

> O Lord, we praise You for this life so well lived and the witness that went out to influence many. We praise You that all who choose to join her can come by the same and only path to God—the cross of Jesus Christ—the singular way to victory over the trials of this life and over the devastation of death.

See you soon, Ms. Muriel!

Listen for the Trumpets of God

Sound the trumpets, Lord, sound the trumpets!
You used this call for Your people Israel
    to follow You immediately,
        in war and in celebration,
        in obedience to Your leading,
    for great blessing and assurance
           of Your Glory among them.

Now teach me to follow Your leading, to hear Your Voice.
Let me hear the silver trumpets,
    which sound alarms of danger,
    which call to worship and celebration,
    which call to move out at the appointed time.

And the one I long most to hear is the very last one—
    done in a twinkling of the eye—
    not sounded by Aaron's sons,
    but by the Angel Gabriel—

The one that calls the dead to rise
    and put on new bodies,
    untarnished by sin,
    wearing at last
    the clothing of Paradise.

An Answer Came ...

*O*ne Sunday night, we heard a moving sermon at our church, from the book of Daniel. Daniel had prayed a desperate prayer, and sometime later, the angel Gabriel showed up to help him. The angel had been delayed, but he assured Daniel that his prayer was heard and had been answered when he first started to pray. This scripture had tremendous meaning to us because of what had happened the previous night.

The Saturday night before this sermon, we sat around our kitchen table with some dear friends who were missionaries from South Africa. My husband and I shared the deep sadness of our hearts with our friends. One of our children had been estranged from us for several months, and we poured out this hurt to these dear saints of the Lord. It was ten thirty at night, and, although the hour was very late, our friends said, "Let's spend some time in prayer about this." And so it was that we all lifted our voices to the Lord, asking for a breakthrough in this important relationship. Our friends cried out to God for help and for restoration; we cried out also, and after a time, the peace of the Lord seemed to settle over us. Our friends left, and we went to bed.

We were in bed but not asleep when, at eleven o'clock, the phone rang. It was our daughter, the child we were estranged from, and she invited us to come to some event at the local university where she was just beginning her freshman year. We were delighted, and, of course, we went. That was the beginning of a rebuilding among us, and the foundation for us to spend a great deal of time with her for the next four years of her college experience. We spent many pleasant hours together at our home, with all of us interacting with Christian friends and missionaries who were frequent visitors.

Among other guests, a young married couple from India actually lived with us for several weeks while they awaited a visa in order to travel to the country where they were to serve. The five of us spent some wonderful times together and became very close as a group. It turned out that this association was a significant link in our daughter's journey toward salvation.

How blessed we were, and how grateful to God that He had so quickly answered our prayer that night when we prayed so desperately for help. Many months later, when our relationship with our daughter was very strong, and after she had made a commitment to Christ, her father decided to share with her the story of our prayers and the quick answer. He told her of our ten-thirty prayer and of her subsequent call at eleven o'clock.

She looked surprised when he told her this story, and then she said, "Well, Dad, it was at ten thirty, while I was driving in my car, that I suddenly had the urge to call you. I just had to wait until I could get to a phone!"

The Day Comes Again

The light has returned!
Darkness has been put away again.
The morning sun streams in the window,
    shining on the written Word,
        and blazing a path of renewed hope.

Your mercies, O Lord, have been renewed again—
    like a continual contract with Your people.
You tell us to remember again Your covenant—
    which You keep for us—
    which we cannot keep.
We remember Whose we are again today.

Yes, Lord, the day has returned
    and delivered hope to my door,
    has renewed my zeal,
    has called me to thankfulness,
        and reminded me again
            of the Light of this world
                and of the world to come.

Lord, that day will come
    when darkness no longer has a turn,
    when Your Radiance and Glory
        light up heaven forever!

But even for now, we who are covered
        by the light of Your salvation
        are daily bathed in Your shining victory
        over the darkness!

The Reservation

When Rachael was a young nurse in training, she very much dreaded beginning the first day she was required to work on the pediatric ward. She wondered how she could manage the emotional challenge associated with seeing seriously ill children. Nevertheless, she resolutely walked into the room of her first patient.

Ralphie was a beautiful little boy, about eight years old. He had bright eyes and a cheerful countenance, which greatly surprised Rachael, since she knew from his chart that he was terminally ill with cancer and not expected to live much longer.

Rachael gave her little patient her most cheerful greeting, and they began to strike up an acquaintance. After the necessary medical talk, Rachael wanted desperately to turn the conversation toward any diversion she could think of for the boy, so she asked him if he would like for her to tell him a story. Ralphie's response was totally unexpected: he told her that he would like to tell *her* a story instead.

"All right," said Rachael, as she sat down beside his bed, very interested to hear the story he seemed so eager to tell her. "You tell me a story."

"Well," he began enthusiastically, "my mother and daddy told me that I'm going to heaven real soon. It's going to be great! They're coming too, but just later, so they want me to go ahead and save them a place."

Rachael choked back her jolt of emotions, and she had absolutely no idea what to say in response to the child's heartfelt story. But before she could form any thought that would be an adequate reply, Ralphie himself continued the conversation by extending a most generous offer to his new nurse.

"Do you want me to save you a place too?"

"Yes!" Rachael struggled to answer without breaking down. "Yes, Ralphie, please save me a place too!"

Rachael is now many years past this encounter with Ralphie. And since that day, she has learned the way to follow Ralphie to heaven, because she herself had a saving encounter with Jesus Christ in the middle years of her life. Now, from the vantage point of her eighty-fifth year, Rachael still thinks of the poignant offer of little Ralphie to "save her a place." Indeed, she is *certain* she will meet him again—as well as the parents who armed their precious child with glorious truth and gave him the vision to look forward to his new life with Jesus.

> At that time the disciples came to Jesus, saying, "Who is the greatest in the kingdom of heaven?" And calling to him a child, he put him in the midst of them and said, "Truly, I say to you, unless you turn and become like children, you will never enter the kingdom of heaven. Whoever humbles himself like this child is the greatest in the kingdom of heaven." (Matthew 18:1–4)

Illegal Parking

$\mathcal{B}$illy was the youngest of five children and the only son in his family. When he was only four years old, his father died suddenly, leaving his mother to eke out a living for him and those of his sisters who still lived at home. She already had a job at the newspaper once owned by her father and then taken up by her brother, but times were hard in general in those days of the early 1940s, and so the family had to be very frugal in order to survive.

It was not just the hard work that kept this family going, but the strong faith of the widowed mother. Her children remembered her getting on her knees each night and asking God for the help she needed to raise her children and provide for them. There were other family tragedies within a relatively short space of time after the death of the father. A beloved aunt died, two grandchildren were stillborn, one daughter's fiancée was killed in a military plane crash that she witnessed, and finally, one of Billy's sisters died of a brain aneurysm at the age of twenty-one. In all these things, the beleaguered widowed mother trusted in God and managed to keep her family going.

As Billy grew up, his love of sports was the consistent interest of his life. Though he played all sports in season, it was basketball which emerged as his favorite. He was a tall young man in a family of short people, and his mother considered this to be a specific answer to her prayer that her son would be tall.

Billy was also a very good student academically and a polite and godly young man. He remained active in his church and took his faith very seriously. Because of these traits and his increasing skills as a basketball player, there began to be some hope that he could go to college on a basketball scholarship. He always assumed he would go to college, but his mother knew that she could not provide any means for this to happen. They had no savings beyond some small emergency money and generally lived from paycheck to paycheck. She knew it would take a miracle of some sort for her son to attend college.

It just so happened that Billy became a very skilled basketball player, the leading shooter on his high school team, which won many games because of his high scoring. His coach was very proud of him and at one point had an opportunity to mention his talent to the basketball coach at Vanderbilt University, a campus about eighty-five miles from Billy's hometown of Glasgow, Kentucky. The Vanderbilt coach said he would send a scout to have a look at Billy's game performance.

With this bit of news, Billy began to assume he would be going to Vanderbilt—and so did all his friends. With all the optimism of youth, he was still largely unconcerned about where the money for college would come from, assuming it would all work out somehow; but not so his mother, who knew these things did not just happen. She had no idea that her son could receive a scholarship to attend college simply because he played a sport. So she spoke to God about this, along with many other issues which routinely called her to prayer.

Billy's senior year in high school featured his finest athletic performance. Not only did he do well, but his team was a leading team in his school's division. This began to attract the attention of various scouts, and true to his word, the coach at Vanderbilt sent a scout to watch Billy's performance at one of the championship play-offs.

Now this is the point at which this story could have a very expected ending: "High school basketball star is scouted by Vanderbilt coach receives some scholarship assistance to attend said university."

The rest of that particular story would also have read: "However, even with some help from a scholarship, basketball star lacks the funds to attend college."

You will be pleased to know in advance that the Billy of this story was, in fact, able to attend and complete college. Miraculously, his mother's prayers were answered. Although, at that time, Billy did not much concern himself with how he would be able to afford to go to college, he looked back at the events of this time in his youth, and with greater maturity, realized that only the Lord could have made straight this crooked path. That said, the rest of the story follows.

When the scout from Vanderbilt arrived at the tournament to scout Billy, he was somewhat late in arriving, and the gym was so mobbed that he was unable to gain entrance at all—until the second half of the game. Meanwhile, during the first half of the game, it became obvious to the opposing team that Billy was the shooter to stop, since his continual scoring was, in fact, winning the game. So by the second half of the game, the opponents targeted Billy with double and triple teaming so that it was pretty much impossible for him to get off a shot at the basket. And this was precisely what the Vanderbilt scout observed when he finally managed to squeeze inside the gym. The scout must have realized that there was some reason to have guards all over Billy; nevertheless, he had nothing concrete and fabulous to recommend to Vanderbilt. The result was still an offer of a scholarship, but it would only cover half of Billy's expenses. *Half* of college expenses was as impossible as *all* of college expenses to this son of a widowed mother.

Time was marching on, and Billy really did not have a Plan B; but it turned out that the Lord had a Plan A, which was already in motion with the Vanderbilt shutout. This "great coincidence" altered Billy's college plans and the rest of his life as well.

Just after the above scouting incident, Billy's high school coach attended the Kentucky State Basketball championship in Louisville. Also attending the championship was the basketball coach from Georgia Tech. These men did not know each other, but it happened that both of them were staying in the same hotel, both had managed to park in a no-parking zone, and both walked out at precisely the same time to see their respective cars being towed. As you can imagine, they got acquainted.

In the course of the conversation, Billy's coach mentioned that he had a very good basketball player, a lead shooter who was also very good academically (a good idea for Georgia Tech applicants). With that last bit of information, the Georgia Tech coach became very interested, so he asked a lot of questions and got the information necessary to check out the young man of their conversation.

The day following the tournament was a Sunday. Billy and his mother were returning home from church when they saw a tall gentleman get out of a car parked across the street from their house and start walking toward them. He introduced himself as the coach from Georgia Tech and asked if he might talk with them. He was invited in and offered lunch, but he declined, opting instead for a glass of sweet tea.

The coach asked if they knew anything about Georgia Tech, to which Billy replied that he had only heard of the song "A Rambling Wreck from Georgia Tech." So the coach began to fill in the blanks about his school, explaining that it was an academically very strong school located in Atlanta, Georgia. He then asked if they would like to come and tour the campus, an offer which they both enthusiastically accepted, making the actual trip several weeks later.

In the meantime, the coach openly shared that Georgia Tech was offering five full scholarships that year for the first time. He told them frankly that all five had been offered, but there was a possibility that one would not be accepted. In that case, he told them, he was prepared to offer it to Billy—a fully paid ride for a college education at a school with a great reputation. It was a grant-in-aid, no debt attached.

It seems hard to believe in our times when students are usually accepted for college admission as much as a year in advance that, in this case, the final decision came on August 19, mere days before the school term started in September. The full scholarship was left open for Billy, and at that late date, he packed his bags and headed for Atlanta, where he spent the next four years on the basketball team, ultimately earning a degree from a first-rate school.

Virtually all people can look into the past to see those fateful crossroads (usually better seen in hindsight), those occasions when they made one choice over another and it changed their lives forever. Billy was no exception in this regard; the career he had, the person he married, the children he had—all hinged on this fork in the road. However, Billy knew that he had not, in fact, made this decision to go to one school over another, to live one life as opposed to another. The decision was made for him when two coaches, who did not know one another, walked out at precisely the same time, meeting only because they each had acquired a minor parking violation and had their vehicles towed. That was the first part of the decision. The second part occurred when another young man, intended to receive a scholarship to college, decided to reject that offer and go elsewhere, leaving the place open for Billy. But the real decision, and all steps related to it, had been made much earlier, known only to God, and perhaps riding on the prayers of a widow on behalf of her son.

Father of the fatherless and protector of widows
is God in his holy habitation. (Psalm 68:5)

Grace, Repentance, Freedom

I have no words, no ability to say,
    no song adequate to praise.
For what can I say about The Cross
    that keeps absorbing my sin,
    and binding me to You, O Lord?

What would be *enough* to say?

I can say this:
    I hate sin.
    I hate *my* sin.
    I hate your sin.

It deceives, separates, brings down, kills, destroys.
Its tentacles reach to the coming generations; it never
stops—
    until repentance turns it back,
    until You, O Lord, are called to the scene
        to spread Your Grace over us,
        to set us free!

Then the righteous will shine like the sun in
the kingdom of their Father. (Matthew 13:43)

No Proof Good Enough

$\mathcal{W}$e all have read about the rich man and the beggar Lazarus in Luke 16. What a reminder about the nature of unbelief. It seems that unbelief is really *rebellion* at its heart. The very prophetic thing which Jesus told in this story was that it would do no good for someone to return from the dead with a warning to others about sin. This Jesus knew this for a certainty, as He already saw the future rejection by those who would know He had returned from the dead. There is no case good enough to persuade us to give up our sins—if we are so determined to keep them, and if we reject the accountability of a Holy God.

When I was in college, one of my roommates was a skeptic regarding faith. She sort of believed, wished she could believe, wanted God to be there in case of trouble, and so on. This, of course, is actually nonbelief. One day when we were in our dorm room, she said rather desperately, "Why doesn't God just come down here and talk with me? Then I would believe."

She looked at me for an answer to this question, thinking that I was the one with the faith. I had no idea how to tell her to have faith, how to explain why I believed without having had a physical encounter with God. But God was faithful to put in my very untrained mind an answer. I told her that even though the children of Israel saw the Red Sea parted, they were only a short time away from worshipping a golden calf that they watched take form in a mold made by a man. Yes, and the story of the resurrection is even more graphic. It is not only in *our* day that those who have not *seen* Jesus reject him; indeed, it was in His own time, when he was, in fact, seen physically by hundreds after he was raised from the dead. *But rebellion considers no evidence.*

As Jesus said to Thomas: "Blessed are those who have not seen and yet have believed." (John 20:29).

The Wedding Rehearsal

$\mathcal{W}$e are the bride of Christ—His church—bought with the ultimate bride price. We are waiting for our Groom to return, to take us to the Wedding Feast of the Lamb—and our new life in eternity.

But while we wait, there are many discouragements along the difficult road of this life. We deal with the sorrow of seeing people who are lost—and are acting accordingly. But we also observe that among ourselves we too fall far short of what we wish to be—and what we wish others in the body of Christ to be. We are disappointed with human frailty, and the struggle seems endless, as we long to be perfected.

But a pastor once painted a picture in the minds of those of us who sat under his teaching. He told us that he had performed many wedding ceremonies as part of the privilege of his pastoral ministry. He also attended many dress rehearsals the day prior to the wedding. They were always interesting, he said. Things had to be worked through, practiced, and learned correctly. It was often very messy. Tempers could flare under the stress of the planning. Participants showed up in various degrees of disarray and confusion. The bride-to-be might have her hair in curlers, and the groom might look similarly undone. When observing this low state of things, you could develop real concerns that the wedding would not come together.

However, according to the pastor, the next day was a different story indeed. No more curlers and jeans, no more ill tempers and disarray of events. But, rather, in the beautiful setting created by exquisite decorations, the bride would arrive in all her radiance and excitement, the groom would be glowing with pleasure at the sight of his bride—all with very little resemblance to the scene of the previous day.

So it is with the church, the pastor concluded. We are still at the dress rehearsal, still trying to get it right, still struggling to overcome the challenges facing us in a world beset by sin and all its consequences. But the Day of our Wedding is indeed coming. And it will be perfect in every way. Our Groom is waiting for us, and He has removed all possibilities of imperfection.

Let us then embrace this rehearsal for the Day of our Wedding. Let us seek the highest and holiest that we can be. Let us love one another with a love that is not of this world and that grows out of a heart surrendered to Christ. For we are His Bride—The Church—and we are headed for the grandest, most glorious wedding there ever was!

Looking to That Day

Gloria in excelsis deo!
Looking toward heaven today—
Passing through the darkness of earth,
    laying down the burdens
        of the condemned world,
            and shouting praise to the Great I Am
                Who has blazed a path of Light
                    to lead me Home!

Remember, my soul,
    your great inheritance—
    imperishable, undefiled, unfading—
        waiting in paradise for you.
The promise that fuels perseverance—until *that day!*

The Snapshot

*J*ohn made a lasting impression on me. I met him when I was sixteen; now I am old, and I still think of him. I doubt that he is still alive, and I wonder what his life was like after I last saw him so many years ago. I wonder if he ever landed on a solid foundation. Yes, I still wonder ... and hope that he found what he needed the most.

John was someone I held in great esteem. He was my supervisor in the college library where I had a work-study job my freshman year in college. He was smarter than most anyone I knew. I was impressed with his thirty-some-odd years, as compared to my especially young sixteen years.

John was a true friend, at least in my view, though I doubt if he considered our association anything that resembled a reciprocal friendship. No, I'm pretty sure that John set out to be my *mentor*. He did it with the best of intentions and always with kindness. I'm sure he quickly realized how little I knew of the world and how little I knew about thinking in general. He wanted to bring me into the world of critical thinking, especially when he realized that I was very convinced of my Christian faith. This, he believed, was just a sign of my uncritical mind soaking up my parents' religion without any examination whatsoever. While this was certainly not entirely true, it *was* entirely true that no one had ever challenged me regarding my faith.

John was an agnostic. He believed it was the only sane position one could take regarding God. I had never even heard the term *agnostic,* and was shocked to think someone could consider this an intelligent position. We had constant discussions on our opposing beliefs, and he asked me question after question, most of which I could not even begin to answer to his satisfaction.

John did indeed accomplish the goal of kicking me into a thinking mode. Never had I encountered challenges on the level dished out by this very intelligent man. I tried to take on these challenges but soon found that I was never up to a conversation with him. When I went back to him to try to answer a question he had earlier posed to me, he was always running ahead—with even greater challenges. I was highly frustrated at times, and I was also upset by the thought that I was not defending God properly. I told God this and asked Him what I was to do about John. What should I say to such-and-such question? All I could think of was to talk to John about what the Bible said. So that was what I did, but John did not believe the Bible.

Another aspect of this ongoing discussion of my freshman year was the fact that I was very concerned about John. I was young and unskilled in apologetics, but I knew that he was missing something important. He was a true brooding intellect, a man of sadness, of restlessness, of something that I could not really identify. I liked John and felt compelled to keep the running conversation about God going, but I always departed our conversations feeling that some wordless darkness was over us both.

Strangely, John seemed to want to engage in these conversations with me, and he would do so eagerly; but he always ended up looking more depressed than ever at the end of them. I was at a complete loss as to what to do. I knew he was like all of mankind in his need to know his Creator, to know the Christ who could save him, but I was a pathetic guide, totally unable to convince him of anything and ending up mentally rattled myself. Sometimes I sensed that John hoped I would be able to talk him into having faith, hoped I could come up with a good-enough apologetic.

John actually admitted that he was drawn to my optimism. He called me *Kid*, and no doubt believed that when I grew up, I would not be so zealous; but for now, he found my innocence, as he called it, refreshing. And I was drawn to John because of the pain I saw in him. I wanted him to know my God and be delivered from the blanket of sadness that I continually sensed in his presence. But meanwhile, he was robbing me of *my* peace, and I began to ask myself if the things he said were true. Was my faith based on thin air? Was I just following the belief of my parents? I felt shredded inside. I couldn't understand why God did not just give me some good answers. I was miserable but doing my best to keep up a good front in John's presence. But after a long, torturous period of mental agony, the Lord was pleased to give me a picture of how things *really* were. It was such a graphic image that it stands crystal clear in my mind these fifty-plus years later.

It was a dreary day, overcast and cold, with the wind actually howling outside. It was a good day to be depressed—if a person were so inclined. I fairly ran from my English class into the warmth of the library, eager to warm up and begin work. I walked into the back where the staff busied themselves with various chores. John was alone in one of the back rooms but not actually busy. He was standing by a large window which stretched across the whole room. He stood sideways to me and was obviously looking out the window, observing the gloomy weather. He did not hear me approach, so my first glimpse of him revealed the look of an unguarded demeanor. I stopped short of entering into his private, dark world, and my mind suddenly took a snapshot of the scene—one that is as clear today as those many years ago. John and the elements seemed to blend into a single dark despair. The great, billowing clouds, the bitter chill, the gloomy overcast sky—and John in front of the window, seemingly an exact match for the menacing weather. In a profound moment, I seemed to see the depth of his hopelessness. And with the same suddenness of this image came the simultaneous words spoken not *by* me, but *to* me from a Voice I could hear in my head and knew was divine: "Is this the one who has troubled your mind?"

Yes, Lord, I whispered inwardly to the One who spoke to me. I was completely startled, overwhelmed by this barrage of truth. I totally got the point!

How foolish I had been! I spoke to myself, following the Lord's admonition to me. How can this man have *any* answers for me? How can this man disturb my peace? I have the Words of Life. I have the joy of my salvation. Dearest, darkest John! He lives with the despair of those who are perishing!

Things were different after that day and that snapshot I received. I no longer cared that I was no match for John's intellect. My joy returned, and my heart was filled with praises for God, who had clearly spoken to me. The sadness remaining was for my dear friend John, a man lost in the darkness of questions with no answers. He knew something was different, that he was no longer able to trouble me with his arguments. He knew my peace and joy had returned—and he even seemed glad of it, for he was a true friend.

As my time at the small college came to an end, I knew I was leaving for another place. John was leaving as well. We would be hundreds of miles apart and guessed we would never meet again. It was very hard to part, for we had formed a bond like that of a big brother to a little sister.

In one of our last conversations, he said to me, "Well, Kid, I would love to meet you again at the end of your college years, to see if you are still standing on your faith. I am convinced that you will change—and to tell you the truth, I would rather hate to see it."

Sadly, we parted, but I thought of him so often in my college years that followed. I saw the graphic image of his despair—forever etched in my mind every time I thought of him—and it broke my heart. How I wanted to see him again and give an updated testimony that Jesus was still the Rock on which I stood, the power that had transformed me and given me the peace that cannot be understood by those who do not know Him. I wanted to invite John, yet again, as an older, more mature person, to partake in life and not death. I prayed for him and hoped for him.

At last my college experience was nearing an end, at least the undergraduate part. It had taken me five years to get a bachelor's degree, primarily because of financial issues and the need to take time out to work more when the money ran low. But there I was—just a few days from graduation—and in a university in South Florida, far from my early start at a local college in Orlando and the experience with John.

It was almost closing time for the college library where I was doing some last research one night. It was nearly ten o'clock at night, and the library was virtually empty. I headed into the book stacks to search for an article I needed. I was rushing, and I almost ran over a man coming from the other direction. I looked up to apologize and found myself looking into the face of my old friend John. How truly shocked we both were—and delighted beyond words! After exclamations of surprise, after hugs, after smiles of true friendship, we exchanged quick updates on our lives.

And then John took my hand and said, almost hesitantly, "Well, Kid, I have to ask. Has your faith held during these years since I last saw you?"

I was almost overcome with joy as I said, "Oh, yes, John! Greater now than then! I am so sure of the reality of God and that He seeks us out to save and to bless us. His hand has been on me all this time."

I don't remember the rest of our conversation, but I do remember that John smiled a sad smile at my enthusiastic response and then said, I think very truthfully, "Well, good, Kid. I'm glad."

I said everything I could to dear John. I knew God had answered his own request, even if he didn't believe in God. He had seen faith withstand the challenge of growing up and encountering many godless people. He had seen the joy of the Lord in another person, and I knew he wished he could have had the same. Of course, it could have been his for the asking, for the bending of the knee before the cross of Christ. I don't know the end of John's story, but I do know the Hound of Heaven was after him. Even a great intellect would have a hard time with the "coincidence" of that meeting—fulfilling John's own wish expressed years earlier.

I never saw John again. I hope with all my heart that he will be among the redeemed with whom I shall spend eternity.

Let Hell Retreat

God, how shall I face the awaking moment
    and keep hell at bay?

Praise be to You, O Mighty God!
Let hell tremble that I am awake,
    armed with Your power
        and not my own weakness.

Let hell retreat before me today
      as I refuse to flirt with disobedience,
      as I reject all sin opportunities,
      as I remain in Your Presence,
      as I give You thanks for all things.

With Your Glory as my constant motivation,
      let that Glory be the weapon that kills despair;
      let despair be cast into the flaming fires
        of hell's retreat!

About Those Leaves …

$\mathcal{S}$arah and her husband were getting old. They were no longer able to keep up with the demands of their home and yard, and things often went undone. They were also on a fixed income and not always able to hire others to do things for them. So they plugged along, doing what they could and choosing not to dwell on imperfect circumstances. And these two were not discontent by any means, for they were followers of Jesus, and they had learned to focus on blessings and live in the joy of the Lord.

Sarah was in a ladies' Bible study at a local church. She was a blessing to those around her, with her cheerful spirit and her frequent praise to the Lord for His goodness. On one occasion when she came to the Bible study, she was so filled with excitement that she could hardly wait to share what the Lord had done for her and her husband. The story went something like this:

It was a Sunday afternoon, and Sarah and her husband returned home after church. Among other things that needed attention at their home was a great pile of leaves, which had accumulated on the roof of the house and in the gutters. They knew this would be trouble, of course, and likely to cause leaks. The situation was evident every time they drove up to their house, but Sarah would absolutely not comment on the problem because she was so afraid that her husband would attempt to get a ladder and remove the leaves. She knew he was unable to do this, and it would be dangerous for him to try. So she made a point of trying to distract him each time they arrived home, and she discouraged him from spending time in the yard. But this particular day, she sighed inwardly, knowing that something had to be done.

After lunch, Sarah took a nap, but not before she spoke to the Lord, asking Him, "Lord, what shall we do about those leaves?" After asking Him, as usual, she decided to not worry about it and proceeded to take her nap. Sometime during her sleep, she thought she heard a great noise outside the house, but deciding it was a dream, she continued to rest peacefully.

When Sarah woke up, her husband was waiting eagerly to tell her the most amazing news. "Sarah," he said with great excitement, "you can't believe what happened while you were asleep! I heard a frightening sound outside, like a great storm. I looked out, and the sun was shining brightly, but the wind was swirling ferociously, almost like a tornado. I started to wake you up because I thought the house might collapse! But then, suddenly, it just stopped. I went outside to see if anything was damaged, and everything was perfectly fine. But guess what! The leaves were blown off the roof and even out of the gutters!"

Sarah looked on steadily as her husband continued. "While I was just staring at the situation, David (the neighbor) came running over and asked me what on earth had just happened. I said I didn't know, except that a big wind came through, so strong that it cleaned my roof and gutters *for* me. He said he had never seen anything like it. 'It was like your own personal wind storm!' he said. He said he had heard a loud noise and came out to see what was going on, and he saw this terrific wind surrounding our house, blowing leaves everywhere. But there was not even a breeze in his own yard—or anywhere else that he could see. 'How is this possible?' he asked me."

Before her husband could say anything more, Sarah replied calmly, "Well, I know how this was possible. Before my nap, I asked the Lord what we were going to do about those leaves, and He just took care of it Himself."

O LORD, my heart is not lifted up;
   my eyes are not raised too high;
I do not occupy myself with things
   too great and too marvelous for me.
2 But I have calmed and quieted my soul,
   like a weaned child with its mother;
   like a weaned child is my soul within me. (Psalm 131:1–2)

Calm and Quietness of Soul ...

Lord, don't let me be lifted up in pride
      by things from inside or outside.
I bow before You sincerely and ask—
      Let me think of You above all.
      Let my mind and my heart
            be fixed on You.
      Let me be occupied with You,
            with my relationship with You—
                  first, above all, in all.

Let me not be occupied with concerns
      which are above my ability to understand;
but let me walk hand in hand, by faith,
      with You, my God.

When I think of the impossible problems,
      my soul feels shattered
            and hopeless;
Then I think of the world and its solutions—
      which are *no* solutions.

So to You I run for shelter,
        asking You to remove these weights
            too great for me to bear,
        these problems
            with no answers.

And I ask You to carve a path
        for me to follow,
and teach me to lean
        on the Everlasting Arms.
Then my soul will be quieted,
        as a little child who walks hand in hand
            with a Perfect Father.

A Child's Story for Adults Too

*O*nce there was a little girl who had beautiful brown eyes. A lot of the people she knew had blue eyes, and she thought blue eyes were much more beautiful. So one night she prayed to God and asked Him to change her eyes from brown to blue. She went to bed very excited because she believed that by the time she got up the next morning, her eyes would be blue. The next morning, she jumped out of bed and ran to the mirror. She was really upset to see that she still had brown eyes. She thought that God must not be listening to her—maybe He didn't really love her after all.

But this little girl grew up to be a woman. She learned a lot more about God, and she understood that God thought about her and planned everything about how she would look—even before he created the world! She didn't worry about her brown eyes anymore.

God called this young woman to leave her home, to go to a country far away so that she could tell others about Jesus. She saved a lot of little children from terrible things, and she told many, many people about Jesus. She was loved and appreciated by so many people, loving them as she loved her own family. But many times this woman's life was in danger. Certain cruel people in this country were always looking for people from other countries who came to speak about Jesus. They would sometimes put them in jail or harm them. They could usually tell who the people from other countries were because they looked different. You see, this country was a country full of people with brown eyes, and anyone with blue eyes was from somewhere else. So people with blue eyes were sometimes put in jail or hurt.

The little girl who once prayed for blue eyes did not get her prayer answered the way she wanted. God knew that someday her very life would be saved because of her brown eyes. And He knew that many people would come to know Jesus because of the witness of this woman. God knew exactly what was best for her when he said no to her request for blue eyes.

[AUTHOR'S NOTE: *This is the story of Amy Carmichael, missionary to India.*]

A Tiny Prayer

A tiny prayer arises
> against mountains of trouble.
A tiny prayer pleads
> against the spreading darkness.
A tiny prayer begs for help
> against endless evil.
A tiny prayer cries to heaven—
> how long, O Lord?

A tiny prayer uttered
> from a not-important voice,
>> but from a helpless one,
>> a powerless one,
> almost too bereft to make sound;
> humbly daring to ask The Great One—
>> and wondering if the prayer is too tiny
>>> in the greater scheme of things—
> thinking it does not deserve to be heard.

Now the tiny prayer leaves the weak mouth,
> drawn upward, invited to heaven;
> it begins to emit the aroma of sweet incense,
>> with purposeful aim
>>> before the altar of the Living God.

The tiny prayer is caught up by heavenly Strength,
> greater than the weak voice,
> greater than the mountains of trouble,
> greater than the spreading darkness,
> greater than the endless evil—

It flies on wings of invitation
>	by way of a vile cross—
>	into the Throne Room,
>	received by the Loving Ears
>		of the Father.

Not helpless,
Not unheard,
Not unheeded,
Answered for the best good
>	of the small petitioner.
Answered at the determined time
>	of the Sovereign One,
>		Whose great and mighty love
>			accepts the tiny prayer.

Go about Your Life ...

$\mathcal{M}$y father was dying a terrible death, and I thought I could not bear it. I was in my thirties, but it seemed all too soon to give up this one who had been my greatest support and friend, the one who loved me unconditionally, the one from whom I had learned so many important things about life.

It was, however, the extent of my father's suffering that was the greatest issue for me, not his imminent death. I knew with certainty that our parting would only be temporary, for Daddy had taught me the greatest truth of all: the reality of the power of Jesus Christ to save my soul for all eternity. I knew that Daddy had long ago been forgiven for his sins, had trusted Christ to save him, and would soon arrive safely in the arms of God. For that same reason, I also was certain of my own future and of the fact that my father and I would have all of eternity to be together. But the horror of watching him struggle to breathe—the result of the malfunctioning of his lungs—was taking its toll on me.

At one point, Daddy was put on a machine which breathed for him. It was a temporary relief from his struggle, but, of course, it would have to be removed at some point. The machine made a steady, rhythmic noise like that of someone gasping for breath—loud and slow. As I stood by him, the machine seemed like a great monster that was holding him captive, torturing him, while at the same time giving him life. But that had to end, and so did his life. In fact, I prayed constantly for the Lord just to take Daddy Home to be with Him.

And after many bouts with the monstrous breather, at last, Daddy was released to God. My tears were ones of relief for him. For a period of time, I was actually rejoicing, postponing the reality of missing him terribly. He was free! I was so happy for him!

So the days passed, and I had my share of grief from just the loss of companionship with my wonderful father. Nevertheless, I also could easily smile as I thought of his journey completed. I knew well what the apostle Paul said he wanted to hear from the mouth of God when he got his call Home: "Well done, good and faithful servant." (Matthew 25:23). I knew that Daddy had heard those words too.

In spite of these comforts I knew from God's word, I found myself left with an emotional association that did not easily let go. It took a while for me to see the pattern that was forming in my thinking. I would find myself returning to those terrible visions of my father's suffering. I would see his face, see his struggle, and hear the loud rhythm of the breathing machine. It would happen during quiet moments, or even unexpected, busy moments. I would quickly try to dismiss the images and sounds of those terrible days, but they would periodically return. I could not seem to totally put it to rest. This continued for two or three years after Daddy had gone to heaven. While it did not happen continually, it just never seemed to be completely gone. I could quickly replace the memory with the words to my father's favorite song, "Heaven Will Surely Be Worth It All." After hearing the words, I would smile to myself, and all would be well for a while. But as time went on, another dimension of the problem emerged.

I began to find myself waking in the night, struggling to breathe! I would dream of the breathing machine, hear it in my sleep, and wake up gasping for breath. Many nights, I found myself leaping out of bed, standing in the middle of my bedroom, trying to get air. Of course, I realized that I really did not have a breathing issue; I was just still struggling with the trauma of having watched my father suffer. I knew I needed to let this go, needed to move on. My father would have been devastated if he had thought I would be left with such issues. I knew this should not be happening.

Somewhere in this fog of unresolved struggle, it finally occurred to me to ask God to help me. As I look back at this after these many years, I cannot imagine why that was not the *first thing* I did. But at last, after one of the episodes of waking up and feeling as if I could not breathe, I prayed.

"Lord, help me to get rid of this terrible memory of Daddy suffering. I know he is with You and not suffering at all. Yet I am stuck with this sorrowful picture."

After praying, I went back to sleep. I continued to ask God for help in the days that followed, whenever the troubling memories haunted me. A few days later, an answer came in an unexpected way.

I had a dream as I slept one night. It was not like the usual foggy, surreal, confused dreams I usually had. It was like a snapshot of reality, and it was very brief. I saw a beautiful scene: a field of gorgeous flowers with majestic mountains in the background. Everything was bright and pristine in appearance. In the middle of the field of flowers my father was sitting in a rocking chair (one of his favorite places to sit). He was young and healthy. He looked better than I had ever seen him in my whole life. He was smiling, and he began to speak to me. He said, "Don't worry about me anymore. I am well now. Go about your life, and I will be waiting for you." That was the end of the dream.

I woke up with an incredible feeling—of I hardly know what. This picture was etched in my mind, and I felt that I had crept into the very edge of heaven through this dream. I knew this was God answering my prayer. He replaced the picture of my suffering father with the reality of his new dwelling place. Daddy sitting in a rocking chair, Daddy amid scenery that was exactly his taste—the flowers, the mountains, the radiant colors, the dazzling, cloudless sky—Daddy at home with God.

My breathing problems ended. My heart settled. My gratitude to God was indescribable—and still is. And I'm guessing that there will be another rocking chair available for me when it is my time.

We Are Listening

When You called me, I was listening;
    I was listening for Your Voice.
When I heard You, I went running!
I've been waiting all this time—
I've been listening, I've been waiting;
    now I'm finally going home!

Lord, You blessed me in this lowland.
Yes, You blessed me even here;
    but I'm ready for the Journey,
        and our meeting face-to-face.
Now You've called me to my Real Home—
    I rejoice to hear Your voice!

Lord, I leave so many loved ones,
    also waiting for Your Voice.
Let them run the race You give them,
    and in every trial rejoice.
Hold them close until You call them—
    keep them listening for Your Voice.

As you call us, we are listening,
    listening for the Voice we know.
One by one we heed Your calling—
    singing, dancing as we go.
Then together we will worship
    when we all have made it Home!

When It Became Real

$\mathcal{B}$arbara was in personal turmoil. She had trouble sleeping, she was anxious to the point of panic at times, and just upset in general. As to what this was about, she was not sure, but since she was even fearful for her husband to leave the room because it sparked dread that perhaps the rapture of the church had come and she was left behind, Barbara began to wonder if she was really saved. She was active in church and had been for years. But all this anxiety ... could she really be secure in the sight of God? And there was also the terrifying incident in which Barbara was driving and heard demonic voices from the backseat of the car—mocking and taunting voices—telling her she would be in hell with them.

At last, Barbara decided to go talk to her pastor about the problem, so she took a lunch hour from her work and dropped by his office. Both the pastor and his wife, who was the secretary, were there when Barbara arrived. She explained her symptoms and anxiety level, as well as her uncertainty of her salvation. The pastor asked her why she was so anxious, and she said she did not know. He decided to take her to the scripture and go through the central gospel message and plan of salvation with her, though she was very familiar with the whole thing. He asked her, step-by-step, if she believed that Christ died for her sins, if she knew she was a sinner and could not be saved apart from the redemption provided by Christ's death on the cross, etc. Yes, yes, yes, she believed all these truths.

In that case, the pastor noted, she must really be saved. Barbara left and went about her life, trying to rest in this assurance. She continued to serve in church in various capacities, but there was an area that she absolutely hated: adult Sunday school. Therefore she managed to teach small children and keep herself out of this arena. But one Sunday, some circumstance arose where she was actually sitting in an adult Sunday school class. It was an unusual situation all the way around, in that Barbara was present and also that the regular teacher of the class had become ill that very day and asked another teacher to fill in. The substitute teacher was totally unprepared since he had just received the request to teach. He admitted to the class that he was unprepared, and told them that he had an exercise he wanted them to do. He said he knew that all of them there were Christians, and he gave each of them a piece of paper and told them to write with the assumption that this would be the last day of their lives and they would be expressing to their children (or other important persons in their lives) the one thing which was most critical for them to know above all else; i.e., their last words to the one or ones they loved the most.

Barbara was not thrilled with this assignment, but she wanted to cooperate. She began to write to her son, her only child: "The most important thing I want you to know is that Jesus Christ died on the cross for your sins so that your soul could be saved. He is the only way for you to be reconciled to God and the only way to heaven. God gave His only Son for you, just as you are my only son." Something then began to happen to Barbara. She started crying. She was overcome by the power of the Holy Spirit. She realized in that very moment that she was being saved, that she really *was* surrendering to God for her salvation. She also knew that this had not happened before. She *really believed* this critical message to her son.

Barbara told her husband what happened as soon as she got the chance. She realized that she also needed to stand before the church and make this public confession, a task that would not be easy, since she had claimed to be a Christian for years, and those in her church had believed this to be true—except for one person. The pastor's wife, who had been present years before when Barbara came to talk to them on her lunch hour, had never been convinced that Barbara was saved.

With considerable courage, Barbara faced her church the following Sunday, making a public confession that she had at last been saved. This time, she *knew* she was saved, and all the doubts and fears were gone. And what a glory to God is this testimony: as she testified to her own son about God's Son, she finally knew God in a saving way.

Danger in the Sandbox

$\mathcal{I}$ was a very small child and lived in our little white house in a very small town surrounded by farms and rural landscapes. It was a great place to live. I was surrounded by grandparents, aunts, uncles, cousins—some next door, others on the various pleasant streets of this early cradle of my life. It was a safer time, and, as a child, I felt safe—*at least most of the time.*

I had a large yard to play in, which constituted the greater part of my world, and I had the amenities of many children of my time. These included two marvelous, tall trees, one of which dropped a rope-and-wood board swing from its great lower branch. The arc of this swing could transport you to magical places—far, far away. Once in motion, it could also trigger grand thoughts about the nature of things, as seen from three years of living.

The other amenity was a wonderful sandbox that seemed to me to be massive in size and scope, a great boarded square with fine grains of sand that were totally unlike all the other Alabama ground of my experience. Dirt that poured like water—that was fun!

Daddy made these things for me, and I used them regularly for serious thinking—for, indeed, play was my job, my work from which I learned the ways of the world. But as is true for children of this age, I did not even begin to grasp how things *really* worked in the world. The laws of physics, and science in general, were years away, and I was still making up my own stories as to cause and effect.

On one particular day, as I was swinging and singing and making up reasons for things, I decided to swing very high. But then I was struck by a cautious thought. You might think the caution would be related to the danger of swinging too high and getting hurt. But no indeed, it was not that. The real danger, in my way of thinking, was that I might just fly away and never see Mother and Daddy again. After all, birds flew away and disappeared to who knows where. *Yes,* I thought, *I better slow this swing down.* In fact, I decided that I would move along from the swing to the sandbox.

Now why should a small child remember such an ordinary day as this one must have been? It was not because of the slight shudder at the thought of disappearing into the sky, because I had considered this possibility on numerous occasions, usually prompting me to slow down. No, it was not the swing, but the *sandbox* that locked this day forever in my memory. Yes, a new concern developed in the sandbox, and it was exponentially more upsetting than the prospect of flying away.

I played happily for some amount of time in the sandbox on this particular day, having learned many valuable lessons about sand, and trying to keep faith with what I already knew. For example, I knew that sand looked like Kool-Aid powder but did not *taste* like Kool-Aid powder. I also knew that you could not wipe your eyes while playing in the sand, or it would create a series of emergencies. You would try to rub it out, but it would only get worse. You would cry, and Mother would make you get out of the sandbox and wash up, and then you would not be allowed to go back right away. And if you got really wild with the sand, you would get an extra hair-washing and a good scolding.

All this I knew and respected by now. But something was different on this day. This time, it was beginning to get dark—definitely a good twilight. No one had called me in yet, and, certainly, I would not go in voluntarily. But the place looked odd in this unfamiliar light. It did not seem quite so safe; a slight dread hung in the air. Nevertheless, I was deep into my own scientific inquiry. It occurred to me to wonder just what could be under the sand of the sandbox. Did this sand just go on forever? I would just dig until this mystery was solved. Well, surprise! At the bottom of the sand was your routine Alabama dirt. No, the sand did *not* go down forever. Science was briefly satisfied until—*until* a really big question popped onto the screen of the three-year-old mind. *What is at the end of dirt? Dirt is at the end of sand, but what is at the end of dirt? Wow!*

This question must be investigated. I guess I was not so surprised about finding the dirt at the end of the sand, but the question about what was at the end of *dirt* seemed a much greater mystery. Why, it could be *anything!* I was excited. I took my little yellow shovel and began the arduous task of settling this issue. I was a scientist without a hypothesis. I dug and dug, and the twilight deepened. Only more dirt and more dirt. My arm grew tired. I began to get a certain ominous feeling, because of the odd light of the sky. It never occurred to me that I could just get up and go inside. The back-porch steps were all of ten feet away from my sandbox. But I stayed, even though the usually cheery kitchen lights were not on, and, in fact, I saw *no* lights anywhere in the house. The multiple windows on the back of the house had black screens, contrasting themselves against the white wood of the house. Without lights, the windows looked like a series of dark eyes, peering into the shadowy outdoors.

And then, without any warning, the most dreadful thought of all leaped into my mind with a sudden force. *What if I am opening up a hole to the devil's house! What if the devil himself escapes and grabs me?*

In a split second, I tossed aside my digging tools and headed for the cover of the house as fast as I could scramble—not brushing off the sand, not picking up my toys dutifully, not doing any of the things I was supposed to do—and casting scientific inquiry to the wind. To make it even worse, I was running toward the menacing eyes of the dark-screen windows and right into the dark mouth of the screen door! By this time, I was crying for help, sure that something dreadful was right on my heels. The surest help I knew was on my lips: "Daddy! Daddy! Daddy!"

The best sight I ever saw was Daddy coming in the direction of my yells and turning on the lights as he came. He didn't seem to mind that I was covered in sand, especially when I explained the imminent danger of the devil seeping right up through my sandbox. Daddy picked me up, sand and all, smiling and giving me words of reassurance.

And it was also very clear that Daddy was not afraid of the devil. No indeed! He marched right out into the danger zone of my sandbox and covered up the hole. He also unhurriedly picked up my digging implements for me and brought them to their proper place in the back-porch toy box. I watched, fearfully at first, then with relief. *That devil will not mess with* my *daddy,* I thought confidently. Daddy just threw the sand right back in his face, and walked off. Daddy joined me back on the porch and gave me another big hug. He told me he was friends with Someone a lot bigger than the devil.

Me too, Daddy. I want to know your Friend. And someday, when I can no longer call you for help, I can call your Friend.

Sand or Rock

Listen to the words of the culture—
Hear the parents teaching their children:

You are great.
You are wonderful.
You can do anything.
You deserve the best.
From tiny child to sprouting adult,
  no action too small or too badly done
   to not cheer on and compliment.
Sand, sinking sand!

You, you, you, they were told;
I, I, I, they concluded.
We must be gods, they said.

You may give a nod to *The God*, they were told.
He is *your* God, after all.
He is there to serve you as needed,
  to cheer you on, to be the Great Approver.
Sand, sinking sand!

They went forth in strength of pride.
They achieved according to their plans.
Their dwellings grew larger, their adult toys more plentiful.
They admired themselves; they competed with one
  another.
They struggled endlessly for power and influence.
Sand, sinking sand!

Emptiness seeping through toys and success,
      the pace must increase to fill nothingness.
Questions raging inside: Is this all there is?
Something is wrong with me.
What does it mean?
Where is the peace when action slows?
And why does *The God* not cooperate
      when I beckon to Him?
Sand, sinking sand!

The house of ego built on sand.
Feel the slipping,
feel the foundation
      plunging into the abyss!
See the futility.
All is being lost.
Watch it sink—
      and rejoice!

Another house, another foundation—
Foundation of Rock.
Built on *The Rock*.

Humility chases pride,
repentance defeats self-worship,
meaning takes hold.
Lay down the toys,
submit to *The God*.

Purpose is born,
following The Christ all the way Home.
Rock, solid Rock.

Over the Kitchen Sink

At a former church, I knew an elderly woman, Evelyn, whose quiet and godly life had an impact on everyone who knew her. Though she had seen many years and was quite frail in body, the Spirit of the Lord in her was so strong that she drew others to her to seek her counsel.

As Evelyn's ministry became more limited in range due to her declining health, the depth of it still remained as long as she was living, for she took the ministry of Jesus to her neighbors when she could no longer drive; and when she was no longer able to walk to visit them, they came to her so that she could continue to bless and encourage them.

Those of us who knew this old saint assumed that she had belonged to the Lord from her earliest days, no doubt born to Christian parents and schooled in the Bible from childhood. But if anyone happened to ask her about how she came to know Jesus, her story was quite different from what would be expected.

After these many years, I don't recall all the details, but I do remember that she was well into her adult years before she began a search to know if there was a God. She struggled with this issue after a Christian she had met began to tell her about Jesus.

Evelyn's days were filled with much activity and responsibility as she raised her children and served her husband. It was very hard for her to find a time to be alone and to think about this issue of God. It seemed that the best quiet time she had during any given day was the time when she stood over her sink, washing the dishes by hand. So this became her thinking time.

One day as she stood over the kitchen sink, dutifully washing the dishes and gazing out the window into her backyard, she began to speak aloud, asking God if He was real, if Jesus was real. Almost at the same moment she uttered this question, her eyes locked onto something outside her kitchen window, something she had failed to see before, something out of season. It was a single flower, rich in color, and blooming like a glorious work of art just a few feet from her eyes.

Evelyn drew in her breath in awe, for she had always had a great appreciation for the beauty of the things around her.

At the same moment, a voice spoke to her quietly in her head; it was a voice distinctly different from her own voice.

"I am the One you are seeking, Evelyn. I am Jesus. I am the One who created this flower, and I am the One who created You."

Evelyn was astonished. She was elated. She was broken.

"Yes, Lord," she whispered. "I am Yours for whatever purpose You may choose to use me, for the rest of my life."

So it was that Evelyn met her Savior that day, because of a beautiful flower oddly blooming out of season. She did indeed serve Him faithfully for many years until He took her Home. And, always, her favorite place to speak to her Lord and spend time with Him was over her kitchen sink, the place where He had shown her the pathway to life.

Robin—Numbered and Noted

I walked in the cool of the morning.
A robin was gathering her manna-worm
    as I approached;
she startled and almost flew,
    but I moved respectfully
        to a wider range around her,
            so her breakfast could be finished.

From the corner of my eye,
    I saw her finish her worm.
Then I looked back at her,
    and she looked at me
        for a long pause.
I smiled as if to a friend.

I wished I could say something nice—
    I wanted to tell her that I would also be
        shopping for my breakfast this morning.
I wanted to tell her that she was a lovely creature,
    made by the same Hand that made me.

I wanted to say that
    just as every hair on my head is numbered,
        the day she falls from the sky will be noted.

Numbered and noted.
    That is the care of the One who created us both.

All Things Redeemed

Carrie slid quietly into the church pew one Sunday evening, still reeling from a recent situation which had badly shaken her. She wanted to sit alone and listen to the message from the pastor, hoping there would be some comfort, some word from God to explain what had happened. She was nineteen years old, and nothing in her experience had prepared her for the events of the past two weeks.

But she was not to be alone this night, for the woman who served as the church secretary suddenly appeared, traveling to the very middle of the row to sit beside her. Carrie wanted to run—or scream—or do something of great protest. But she sat motionless, not even glancing up at her seat companion.

She had known Mrs. Miller for the past three years, and the woman was much more than just the church secretary. She worked tirelessly with the various youth activities and seemed to have a hand in all things good which took place at Carrie's church. Mrs. Miller was well known to all the young people as a former missionary of the not-so-distant past. Her husband had died on the mission field, and she returned to the United States and became a stalwart of this local church. Indeed, Carrie had a very close relationship with Mrs. Miller, since she was the sponsor of the young women's mission organization, of which Carrie was the president. Therefore, they had planned many outreach activities together and sometimes traveled to other cities to attend various conferences or to participate in mission work. There was no one in the church whom

Carrie admired more than Mrs. Miller. But on this particular Sunday night, Carrie wanted nothing to do with the older woman.

Mrs. Miller chatted in a friendly manner as they waited for the service to begin. Carrie could find no words to respond. Mrs. Miller then picked up Carrie's Bible, which was on the pew between them. She commented that it was pretty dog-eared and that was a good thing. Carrie still could not bring herself to look at her.

The service began, and Carrie felt suspended in some other realm the whole time—through the songs, through the preaching. She heard nothing, she felt nothing—except the urge to escape. She planned to bolt out of the church as soon as the last amen was pronounced. But even in Carrie's haste, Mrs. Miller made a faster move. She picked up Carrie's Bible and announced that she wanted to have it recovered for her—in genuine leather. The young woman objected, insisting that she did not *want* it recovered. Her father had given it to her, and she wanted it just as it was. She tried to be as firm as she could muster in saying no, but Mrs. Miller had the Bible under her arm and was off and heading out of church.

Carrie was so devastated that she thought she might just pass out from some emotion she had never known. What was it? Anger? Yes, certainly that, but it was much more. It was profound hurt and profound lack of understanding. It was deep and wordless. It was a time when she was forced to take a giant leap into adulthood, leaving a lot of innocence behind.

Two weeks prior to this event had been the beginning of great excitement for Carrie. She was leaving town with her dear Mrs. Miller and another girl in the youth group. They were headed from their homes in Orlando to go to Miami, where Billy Graham would be speaking to the Baptist World Alliance. This was a very big deal to the young woman for many reasons. It was a six-hour drive to Miami from her home in Orlando, and it was to be a three-day conference. She was very eager to see and hear Billy Graham in person. She was also eager to spend time with Mrs. Miller, as they had done several other times, but never for this long. And they had another purpose as well. Phyllis, the girl going with them had a myriad of problems and really needed encouragement. Mrs. Miller and Carrie were committed to seeing that Phyllis felt included by and important to them. They were going to help her overcome her discouragement, and they intended to have a great time as Christian sisters, all of them together—or so was the plan.

The trip to Miami was very pleasant, filled with goodwill and building Phyllis up, showing her a good time, listening to her, laughing, singing—a great start. That night was the opening of the alliance. It was in a large stadium, and Billy Graham was the first guest speaker. They were all greatly blessed by the whole evening. Tired and happy, they headed back to their hotel on Biscayne Boulevard. It was a tall building, and they were staying several floors up.

But even as they were traveling to the hotel, Carrie began to feel very ill. She said nothing, hoping it would pass; but when they arrived back at the hotel, she finally said that she did not feel well and would just stay up a while, being very quiet, and mostly staying in the bathroom. She urged Mrs. Miller and Phyllis to go to bed and assured them that she would be fine. She did not honestly know if the two of them stayed in the room or not, since they had reserved two rooms, but her guess was that they did not. In any case, Carrie spent the night in the bathroom, sicker than she could ever remember up to that time. She kept the door closed, however, and made a commitment to not groan or make any noise. She heard no sound from either of her companions throughout the night and assumed they were in the other room getting some rest.

The next morning, Carrie was weak and dehydrated, very close to passing out, as she soon realized when she finally tried to drag herself out of the bathroom and to a bed. But when she emerged from the bathroom, she was surprised to find Mrs. Miller dressed, as if ready to leave, though it was still early in the morning. Phyllis was nowhere to be seen, so Carrie presumed she was in the other room. Mrs. Miller gazed at Carrie unsympathetically—in fact, Carrie thought in her daze, she seemed *angry*. Carrie fell on the made-up bed and tried to speak to Mrs. Miller. She said she hoped Mrs. Miller had passed the night with good sleep and that she had not been disturbed. Mrs. Miller said that indeed she had not been disturbed, but the fact was that their trip and purpose for coming was now ruined completely.

Carrie had a hard time following her words. For one thing, they were harsh and condemning, and this tone was beyond her comprehension, not at all the kind, loving woman she knew so well. Also, she could not understand what Mrs. Miller meant when she said that their trip was ruined. Carrie's mind was very foggy, and she was so weak that speaking almost took too much energy. She tried to fathom what Mrs. Miller was talking about. Meanwhile, Mrs. Miller continued to chide Carrie as if she had done some outrageous thing as a personal affront to her.

Finally, Carrie understood that Mrs. Miller thought her illness was putting a damper on their planned day, and everything had to be changed because of this. Furthermore, it was now very clear that she was extremely angry about the whole thing. Though Carrie was continuing to have a sense of unreality, she began to reassure Mrs. Miller that the plans should proceed as intended. Mrs. Miller and Phyllis should go on to the conferences as planned, and Carrie would simply remain in the room and try to regain her strength. If Mrs. Miller would just leave her some water, she explained, she would be all right. She tried to sound positive, tried to rise above the terrible weakness she still felt even as she was lying down.

But this would not do, Mrs. Miller informed her. They would indeed not be attending the conference, but would be going home. Carrie was to get up immediately and pack her bags. At this point, Carrie honestly thought she was not hearing this right; she was totally dumbfounded, thinking she must be dreaming all this up. Surely, Mrs. Miller was not mad at her for being ill! And surely she must see that Carrie was too sick to travel. Carrie tried again to reason with her.

"Please, Mrs. Miller, you and Phyllis just go ahead, and let me rest here today. I feel sure I will be fine in a few hours."

This was actually wishful thinking, since Carrie never remembered being so sick and so weak. She had no idea what the real problem might be or when she would be better, but she knew she would not be able to walk the considerable distance to the car. This would have involved walking down the long corridor of the hotel from their room to the elevator, going several floors down, walking through a large lobby, crossing the street, and walking another distance to the car.

Carrie continued her plea, even in the face of Mrs. Miller's rising anger. Her face was red and she had a look Carrie had never seen. The young woman was really beginning to be shaken. About this time, Phyllis knocked on the door and entered the room. She had no idea that Carrie was so sick, and she quickly became confused as she observed Mrs. Miller's demeanor and Carrie's helpless condition. She gave Carrie an inquiring look. Carrie explained to Phyllis that she was sick but would be okay, and she wanted the two of them to go on to the conference.

But at this point, Mrs. Miller exploded with anger. She told Phyllis that Carrie had ruined their trip and that they were all going home, no more discussion. She turned to Carrie and ordered her to get up and pack her clothes. Carrie said again that she didn't think she could stand up.

As the tension mounted and Phyllis looked as if she would break down, Carrie tried to cooperate. She slid out of the bed and crawled to her suitcase. Phyllis quickly began to try to help her get her things together, but Mrs. Miller stopped her cold.

"Leave her alone," she scolded angrily. "She can pack her own things. You go get your things together."

Phyllis gave Carrie another look of desperation. She must have thought that Carrie had done something beyond terrible to bring out this new person neither of them knew. Phyllis dutifully went back to the other room to pack.

Carrie managed to sit on the floor, put on a pair of shorts and a top, and stick her feet into her flip-flops. She crawled around to gather her clothes and finally got everything into the suitcase. Mrs. Miller continued to growl her dissatisfaction, but Carrie had no energy to say anything further. She could not make sense of this and was virtually in shock by this time.

Phyllis returned, and Mrs. Miller ordered the young women to march on toward the car. Carrie tried to stand up. She felt faint, but managed to get out the door. Fortunately, the long corridor of the hotel had a handrail, and she held on to it as she tried to stay on her feet. She told Mrs. Miller that she could not manage her suitcase, which angered the woman further, but, finally, she let Phyllis carry Carrie's suitcase. Even so, Carrie had to sit down before they got to the elevator—just to keep from passing out. More anger. They got on the elevator, and Carrie sat on the floor for the ten-story ride down, unable to stand.

They reached the lobby, and the elevator door opened. Carrie saw again the distance to the door in this very old and once-elegant hotel. It looked like the length of a football field to her—and no handrails. She told Mrs. Miller she did not believe she could go that far. But Mrs. Miller ordered her on, so she continued to try. Somewhere on the journey, Carrie lost consciousness and collapsed on the floor. She thought later that Phyllis must have caught her to give her an easier landing. When she came around, some of the hotel personnel were standing over her. She heard one of them say, "We'd better call an ambulance. She needs to be in the hospital."

"I am taking her to the hospital," Mrs. Miller told them.

More total confusion for Carrie as she was helped up and escorted to the door by some kind person in the lobby. At the door, Mrs. Miller took her by the arm, apparently to shake off the hotel staff and to assure them she would take it from there. But when they got outside, she let go of Carrie as they started to cross the major thoroughfare of Biscayne Boulevard. Phyllis was running ahead with the suitcases, thinking Mrs. Miller was covering Carrie.

It was at this point that some survival instinct overrode Carrie's need to be respectful to her elder. She grabbed a light pole near the edge of the street and told Mrs. Miller emphatically that she was not going to go into the street without some help. Mrs. Miller turned around and grabbed her arm, rushing them across, with Carrie leaning heavily on her out of intense weakness. It was only thanks to God that she made it across. She clutched Mrs. Miller tightly to be sure that she would not suddenly drop her and leave her for dead. At this point, Carrie felt that she had been caught up in a living nightmare and had no idea what to expect next.

Each scenario seemed to become more unbelievable than the last. Carrie lay down in the backseat of the car and braced herself for the six-hour drive home, praying that Mrs. Miller would stop if she had to go to the bathroom again. Then came the next shock. Mrs. Miller did, in fact, take her to a hospital, ordering her out of the car when they arrived at the emergency room. An aide brought a wheelchair after seeing Carrie struggle to stand. She was taken in and placed on a stretcher, while some clerk followed her to get details of identity and insurance.

In a fairly short time, Carrie was examined and an IV was administered. Before she could get a word from the doctor, Mrs. Miller announced that she and Phyllis would be going to get something to eat while Carrie was being treated. This was a little frightening to Carrie, but she was also glad to be away from the disapproving glare and mean words. Phyllis stood speechless and looked confused through the entire event. Carrie felt so sorry for her. She was as shocked as Carrie and could not imagine what this was about. But Mrs. Miller and Phyllis picked up their purses and started out. Mrs. Miller also picked up Carrie's purse. Some caution inside Carrie caused her to reach and take it back, saying she might need it while they were gone.

Soon after the attending physician administered Carrie's IV, she fell into a deep sleep, for how long she did not know. When she awoke, the doctor said they decided to let her sleep while the IV did its work. They further said they thought she should be admitted for more fluids and tests, but since she was out of town and was going directly home (according to Mrs. Miller before her departure for lunch), they would trust that she could sleep comfortably on the trip, then go to her doctor at home. They said she was severely dehydrated, and it could be something more than just a nasty virus. She was released.

By this time, Carrie was not as weak as earlier—at least not to the point of passing out, but she was light-headed and the slightest exertion exhausted her. She walked into the lobby of the hospital to see if she could find Mrs. Miller and Phyllis. She realized pretty quickly that she was still not up to much of a walk, so she sat down to look around but did not see either of them. She sat for a considerable amount of time, wishing desperately that she could lie down again. The chairs were plastic bucket chairs, and the temperature of the room was far too cold for her shorts and flip-flops and still weakened condition. She waited for what seemed an eternity, wondering how a meal could take so long.

Finally, the awful truth began to dawn on her. She realized that several hours must have passed since Mrs. Miller and Phyllis had "gone to lunch." After all, she had slept in the ER for a long time, and now she had been sitting in the waiting area for at least an hour. In spite of everything that had happened prior to this, she was having a hard time accepting yet another terrible truth. *They were not coming back.* This hardly seemed possible to her, but by that point, she knew it must be true.

She had very little money with her, and, of course, no credit cards in those youthful days. Her suitcase with her clothes and everything else was in Mrs. Miller's car. Only by the grace of God did she even have her purse. She had never been to Miami, had no idea what hospital she was even in. A horrible feeling began to come over her. She prayed desperately for the Lord to show her what to do.

She saw a line of pay phones across the room and knew this was her only connection to home. She managed to walk to the phones but realized she was still too weak to keep standing, so she quickly found a nearby chair to rest again. She then was able to pull the chair over to the phone so that she could sit down after dialing. She made a collect call home, since she had very little change to pay for a longer call.

Carrie's mother answered the phone and quickly agreed to accept the charges. Carrie knew her mother was near panic just from getting a collect call from her. To make it worse, as soon as Carrie heard her mother's voice, she began sobbing with relief and upset. Her mother was frantically trying to find out what was wrong, but Carrie could barely speak for crying. She finally told her mother, between sobs, that she was all right, but felt sure this was not believable to her mother, considering the delivery of the message.

At last, Carrie was able to speak and told her mother what had happened. Her mother also began crying. When her father heard the commotion and came to see what was going on, her mother tried to tell him, but she was so upset that he did not understand what she meant. He grabbed the phone and tried to find out from Carrie what was wrong. Carrie retold the story, and her father was beyond distressed. He responded with tremendous anger, and then, calming down, told her to give him the number of the phone from which she was calling. He said he and Carrie's mother would discuss what they would do and call her back. Her job was to find out the name of the hospital where she was in Miami.

Carrie did as her father asked, still too weak to walk far without almost fainting. But she got back to the phone area and waited in a chair for the return call from her parents. Her mother soon called and told her that she had a cousin in Miami, whom she had not seen for years. She had called her and asked if she would come and get Carrie and take her to her home until they could come get her.

Carrie's cousin, unknown to her until that moment, picked her up within the hour and took her to her home, where she was treated graciously, given food and clothes, and allowed to rest. She slept for almost an entire day, only waking for water and soup. She then began to recover her strength, but it was three days before they judged her strong enough to travel.

It had been decided between her cousin and her parents that it was best for them to not come down to get Carrie, since they would just be extra guests in a small place and would need to stay overnight to travel back. Also, they had never been to Miami and had no confidence they could successfully navigate the area. Instead, the cousin would lend Carrie the money for a bus ticket, and she would go home without more complicated plans. (In those days, it was safe to travel on a bus.) So the plan was implemented, and Carrie made the several-hour journey home on the bus, after the much-needed rest and recovery time she had received at her cousin's home.

Carrie sat and stared out the window of the bus, and thought long and hard about the past days, now with a clearer mind. But she could not make sense of anything that had happened, no matter how she tried. She had not disturbed Mrs. Miller, had not complained during her illness. Carrie had never before gotten ill when they traveled together, so there was no history of Mrs. Miller's response to health-related problems. Carrie knew she had always been reliable and responsible in working with Mrs. Miller, and, as far as she knew, they had no issues whatever. She had never seen this side of Mrs. Miller, and it still seemed impossible that this whole thing had even happened. Furthermore, how could Mrs.

Miller have just gone off and left her desperately ill in a city far from home, taking her suitcase, and not even telling her that she was leaving! Carrie did not know what to feel. She was numb.

When Carrie got to the bus station in Orlando, her mother and father were there. They all cried again, and her parents were both almost too angry to act sanely. Her father said that Mrs. Miller had delivered her suitcase to their house shortly after Carrie called. Timewise, this meant she had to have left the hospital and come straight back to Orlando, with no intention of returning to the hospital. She had no explanation for Carrie's parents except to say that she was too sick to travel, so Mrs. Miller had left her in the hospital. Carrie's father was furious with Mrs. Miller. He said many things to her, but the one Carrie remembered most was his angry comment: "Mrs. Miller, if you were a man, I would give you a good whipping right here in my front yard."

This incident took a significant toll on Carrie and her family. Her father went to talk to the pastor about it, probably expecting that something would be done to address Mrs. Miller and what she had done. However, it was a dead issue at church. The pastor did not exactly disbelieve Carrie's father, but he was so astonished that he thought there was something that they were all not understanding about the situation. Carrie never knew whether he talked to Mrs. Miller about the matter. He did not talk to Carrie about the event, except to say how sorry he was that she had been so sick; Carrie never mentioned it to him, either. She could almost understand the pastor's lack of action, because even she could not then, or many years later, even begin to unravel such a great mystery—a personality as changeable as that of Mrs. Miller. She had been, after all, the kindest, godliest, quietest, gentlest person most of them at church had ever known.

Carrie's father left the church, and her family was divided by this. He was so distraught that he was not able to accept that the pastor would do nothing in response to what had happened to Carrie. He went to a smaller church down the road and did not look back. By this time, his health was very bad, and, often, he was not able to attend any church. Carrie's mother was also very upset, but neither she nor Carrie said anything further about the church's lack of responsibility in taking the matter further. It was dropped for all time. Carrie and her mother continued to attend the church of Mrs. Miller, and did not hold any grudge against the pastor or church officers. No one, in fact, had been told about the matter except the pastor, so no one else could have been held accountable for taking any action.

As for Carrie, she was young and flexible. She recovered quickly from most things, and, if you had asked her at that point, she would have said the whole nightmare was over with. However, that did not prove to be true. On the very night that Mrs. Miller took her Bible, she was actually worse off emotionally than when the incident first happened. It seemed that a creeping doubt had invaded her mind. She felt disconnected from her Christian family. She found herself wondering what people were *really* like. Who could be counted on if not her wonderful Mrs. Miller? Carrie continually revisited the incident in her mind and tried to make some sense of it, tried to find some logic or reason as to how it could have happened. She reviewed her own behavior until she was weary of her own thinking. She honestly could think of nothing she had done to upset or trigger such a reaction. She found herself beginning to think cynically toward her fellow Christians. She was drifting from them and, in some sense, from her faith—though she could not have told you either of these things at that time.

Mrs. Miller returned Carrie's Bible, all newly covered and looking very unfamiliar. It seemed anathema to Carrie, and she did not want to even open it again. A gift from her father—now totally spoiled, in her mind. All this was just part of the slide downhill for Carrie.

Fortunately, Carrie was about to leave for her junior year of college in a nearby town—but it was too far to return to her home church on Sundays. She was given a wonderful send-off by the church leaders, and was encouraged by them, shown love by them, and all seemed well on the surface. But she was very sad. There seemed to be a hole in her soul. In a very definite way, she wanted to escape this church that had meant so much to her.

Many things happened in the year that followed, and Carrie gradually began to drop the obsessive thinking about Mrs. Miller and the terrible incident. She was moving on and forgiving and forgetting. She had a new church, a small mission church which she dearly loved. She was busy with school, work, and church, and the past seemed to be laid to rest—but not really. She was not the same, in some undefinable way.

The following summer, Carrie made the decision to attend summer school and not go home. She moved into a new dorm, much larger and more modern than the dear old dorm she had lived in during the past two semesters. She didn't particularly like this new look and missed her old dorm, with its great character of architecture and ancient familiarity. Now she was in a newish building with very long corridors and very impersonal looks. But at least she was not in the same arena with Mrs. Miller back at home, as she sometimes consoled herself—thereby proving that it was still on her mind.

Carrie worked at the front desk in this new dorm, usually the evening and night shift. As part of her duties, she was to walk down the long hallways of each floor and check to see that the doors to the outside were locked for the night. The first night that she carried out this assignment, she had a very odd experience. Something did not look right about the corridor. It looked very frightening, though nothing could account for this. She found herself rushing through this duty, trying to get it over with as soon as possible. By the time she had covered two floors and four corridors, she was fairly running—and close to panic. She could not imagine what was wrong and assumed it might be because most of the rooms were unoccupied for the summer, and it was like a deserted building. She did not encounter even one student as she locked up. But nevertheless, she was really being ridiculous, she told herself. However, the next afternoon, she found herself dreading the lockup—long before it was to happen. And again, she began to take on fear as she walked (or ran) the corridors to lock up. Her heart was pounding, and it seemed as if she might just die. The third night, the reaction could have better been described as terror.

Carrie was absolutely dumbfounded by what was happening. Nothing like this was part of her experience, and it was totally irrational, as she repeatedly told herself. Finally, it occurred to her to pray about this. So she desperately put her petition before the Lord as she tried to get to sleep after the third harrowing night of thinking she might die just from walking through the halls of the dorm.

"What is wrong with me?" she pleaded with God that night. "Please help me!" She thought she must be losing her mind but was totally not comfortable with sharing this with anyone. It was just between her and God.

Sometime during the night after that prayer, she had a dream. It was terrifying. In her dream, she was moving down a very long and dark hallway that seemed to never end. It was not the new and modern dorm; no, it was a vaguely familiar older hall, with carpet from another era. She was clinging to an iron handrail on the wall, just to stay on her feet. The darkness was closing in on her in the dream, and she thought she could not escape this place. She would die here; or so she thought in the dream. She heard an evil voice behind her—scolding, threatening, and gaining on her. She was almost unable to move, yet something was coming for her. It was a true nightmare.

She woke up, still terrified. But even as she was coming into full consciousness, she began reconciling the past with her present horror. It was the hotel in Miami! The carpet, the long corridor, the handrail, the rasping voice of Mrs. Miller insisting that she keep moving toward the elevator. And now the long corridor of the dorm. It was the only connection—just the long corridor—and it was taking her back to the dreadful days of the previous summer.

Only by the power of God was she able to break this connection. The Lord had sent her a dream, and knowledge is power. She prayed her way up and down the halls of the dorm for the next few nights, and the panic gradually subsided, never to return. But she also knew that there was work to be done in her soul. She asked God to wash her clean of any future associations with the experience in Miami. She asked Him to help her *truly* forgive Mrs. Miller, whether or not the woman ever said she was sorry, and whether or not Carrie ever understood why Mrs. Miller had done such a terrible thing.

Indeed, Mrs. Miller never did apologize, and Carrie never did understand. She will not know the answer in this life. Of course, she never trusted Mrs. Miller again, nor did she have to be in a position to do so. She only saw her in passing when she sometimes returned to her home church. At times, she could almost pity her, for something was terribly wrong in her soul—a darkness that few had seen. But she was a fellow human being, even one who was supposed to be a sister in Christ. Compassion had to replace bitterness, or the darkness would be all over Carrie's life as well.

As Carrie looked back on the incident from a much-older age, she wished she had taken the initiative of going to Mrs. Miller and asking her to please explain to her what had happened on that fateful trip, what had bothered her so very much, what her reasoning had been—and how they could have truly been restored together. But it was not to be, for she was not that mature, and this thought had never occurred to her at the time. Also, she would have probably thought it to be disrespectful to approach someone more than twice her age with plying questions.

It is also clear that no church should have let such a serious issue go without some investigation, and without church discipline if the story were substantiated. Carrie could have gotten dear Phyllis to relate the story from a third-party view, since she had witnessed the whole thing, but on thinking of this, Carrie decided Phyllis was too fragile to draw into any situation where she would have controversy swirling around her and would have to take a stand with one person or another.

But a greater good came forth from this wrenching experience. In the healing of Carrie's deep wound, the Lord taught her lessons so important that she ultimately counted it worth the whole ordeal. He showed her once and for all that it is not man in whom she could place her trust.

> But Jesus on his part did not entrust himself to them, for he knew all people and needed no one to bear witness about man, for he himself knew what was in man. (John 2:24–25)

Carrie was never to associate the wicked actions of any human being with the character of her great and wonderful God. She was never again to be shaken by mere man; no one could possibly represent the Lord adequately, and she knew that she herself would be the first one to fail to do so. No cry of "hypocrite!" would fall from her lips as an excuse to remove herself from the fellowship of Christians. She realized that she could not be trusted any more than Mrs. Miller. She hoped she would never do what Mrs. Miller had done—or anything like it—but she knew she was capable of great sin and could also cause someone to stumble in his or her faith. She resolved to look to God alone for perfection, and also to never paint all Christians with the broad brushstroke of the sins of one.

The other great lesson, of course, was the obvious one of forgiveness. Over a period of time, it became so clear to Carrie: When you never receive an apology, when you never understand why you have been mistreated, and when justice never comes; still, our Lord says to let no bitter root grow that will not only enslave the offended, but will also spread poisonous harm to all who are touched by its self-concerned tentacles. Ultimately, Carrie had to let the offense fall away, through the power of God, and be replaced by compassion for a fellow sinner, Mrs. Miller.

These lessons were taken to heart at an early age, and were to be rehearsed again and again over many decades of needing to forgive. God had redeemed evil and turned it into a lifetime of good. Let God be praised in every trial, for He is able to redeem all things!

Taking Offense: The Optional Responses

An unrighteous thing was done to me.
I am offended. I am hurt.
I was not shown respect.
It should not have happened.
It was not fair. It was not right.
It was against the laws of God.

I defend myself to the offender.
Maybe I defend myself to others as well.

I respond with the certainty of my truth,
     and with correction.
The offender needs to account for the wrong done,
     and I am the one to whom he or she must account.

I will draw some boundaries;
I will have the last word,
     and if repentance is not shown,
          I will walk away from this one.
And begin the journey of the bitter root.

An unrighteous thing was done to me.
I am offended. I am hurt.
I was not shown respect.
It should not have happened.
It was not fair. It was not right.
It was against the laws of God.

I do *not* defend myself directly,
     but the defense is large in my mind.

If walking away looks too harsh to others,
    I will instead withdraw with aloofness and passivity,
        so I can say I have done nothing wrong.
    Indeed, I am nobly overlooking the offense,
        and being nice in return.
But not really.

I do not face the offender,
    but I avoid and resent.
        Or I pretend all is well,
            but show by my actions that all is *not* well.

A bitter root begins to grow.
The problem is widened; a relationship is broken.
A deadly journey begins for the offended one.

An unrighteous thing was done to me.
I am offended. I am hurt.
I was not shown respect.
It should not have happened.
It was not fair. It was not right.
It was against the laws of God.

I examine myself to see if I am too easily offended.
Was the offense biblically wrong, or just wrong in my eyes?

I take the matter before the Lord, with an open heart.
Is my pride the real issue?

I ask God to move me to forgiveness and mercy
    toward a fellow sinner—
        remembering all the times I have offended;
        remembering the mercy of God extended to me.
I release the offense to God.

I determine that it is not worth
      bringing up as an issue.

I determine to love the offender
      and overlook the offense,
          now and in the future.

I am released to walk in freedom.

An unrighteous thing was done to me.
I am offended. I am hurt.
I was not shown respect.
It should not have happened.
It was not fair. It was not right.
It was against the laws of God.

The offense is clearly in the realm of sin,
      and not just a challenge to my pride.

I pray for wisdom.
I pray for love to abound over the offense.

I examine my own heart to see the log in my own eye.
I remember when I have acted out this same sin,
      perhaps in some other form, but the same in principle.

I go to the person, only after my heart is right before God.
I speak gently as someone who loves.

There is no strife, no intensity in my voice.
There is no condemnation or self-righteousness
      in my speech or in my heart.
There is no self-defense
      in my speech or in my heart.

I tell the offender the problem and confess
    any sin I have in the matter.
I listen to the response without rising to argue
    if I still disagree.
Insofar as it is up to me, I will be at peace.

The offender is convicted and responds biblically.
I rejoice with this one that the issue
    can be laid open, confessed by both,
    and that God forgives all who repent.

A sin is turned back, and no bitter root forms.
I will let go of this offense and not hold it against the offender.
I will continue to pray over it until all roots of it are gone.
I will thank God that He has also forgiven me for every offense
    I have ever committed against Him.

An unrighteous thing was done to me.
I am offended. I am hurt.
I was not shown respect.
It should not have happened.
It was not fair. It was not right.
It was against the laws of God.

The offense is clearly in the realm of sin,
    and not just a challenge to my pride.

I pray for wisdom.
I pray for love to abound over the offense.

I examine my own heart to see the log in my own eye.
I remember when I have acted out this same sin,
    perhaps in some other form, but the same in principle.

I go to the person, only after my heart is right before God.
I speak gently as someone who loves.

There is no strife, no intensity in my voice.
There is no condemning or self-righteousness
      in my speech or in my heart.
There is no self-defense
      in my speech or in my heart.

I tell the offender the problem and confess
      any sin I have in the matter.
I listen to the response without rising to argue if I still disagree.
Insofar as it is up to me, I will be at peace.

The offender is *not* convicted and does *not*
      accept any guilt or responsibility for the offense.
I am sad, but I will not take up anger or indignation again.

I will not pity myself because I have been rebuffed.
I will not treat the offender as any less of a person.
I will pray that a bitter root will not take place in the heart
      of this one who does not bend—or in my own heart.

I will trust the matter entirely to The Judge of All the Earth,
      and relinquish all outcomes to Him, the One who alone knows truth.
I will choose love, and I will not become prisoner to any injustice—
      I will do this by the grace of God.

The Blessing

$\mathcal{M}$y husband and I were in another state for a few days, and I had such back pain that I was forced to seek medical help. This is how I happened to be sitting in the waiting room of a doctor's office when an elderly lady came from her doctor's exam back into the waiting area. She pushed a wheeled walker that also had a seat and a rack for carrying her purse or other things. She paid her bill and turned slowly toward the door to leave. She said quietly to the receptionist, "I wonder if you might open the door for me so I can push through." She was obviously alone on this visit to the doctor.

I was sitting very near the door and quickly got up, saying I would be glad to open the door. She smiled gratefully. I stepped out with her and realized that she would need to fold her walker and put it in the trunk of her car, a task that seemed a lot to ask of her small, bent frame, so I said I would love to walk her to the car and help with the walker. She gave me a kind smile, with both her eyes and lips, and said she would much appreciate it. After a few steps, she stopped. Balancing herself with her left hand on the walker, she offered her right hand to me in greeting, introducing herself as Elanna. We squeezed hands, and I told her my name and said that I was pleased to meet her. She thanked me again for helping her.

It was raining lightly, but Elanna could not hurry, and neither of us minded the drizzle. She opened the trunk of her car, and I folded the walker up and placed it appropriately. Such a radiant face and lovely smile rewarded me many times over. I closed the trunk and said, "Good-bye, Elanna, it has been a pleasure to meet you."

> As I walked away, I heard her quiet voice sending some powerful words my way, pronouncing a blessing on me from the Word of God: The Lord bless you and keep you; the Lord make His face to shine upon you and be gracious to you; (Numbers 6:24–25).

> I turned around to see her gentle face for the last time, and without hesitation, finished the blessing in return to her: The Lord lift His countenance upon you and give you peace. (Numbers 6:26)

Two strangers, likely to never meet again, touching lives by means of a profound, shared knowledge. Yes, probably not meeting again here, but surely meeting *there* in the presence of Him who bound us together.

The Word of the Lord: It Is Enough

O God, my Father,
this morning brought a dread of certain realities,
    a fear upon awakening,
    the remembrance that terrible things are wrong.
But I took this burden that comes
    between evening and dawn,
        and I went into the chamber of Your Word—
            to inquire of the Only Wisdom under the sun.

And with the first sentence of Your written Voice,
    You spoke relief, You spoke comfort—
        with only these simple words to Ezekiel:
            The Word of the Lord came to me ... (Ezekiel 6:1)

That was the calling back to peace,
    the remembrance of what is true,
        of how things will finally resolve ...

The Word of the Lord!
It spoke worlds into being;
It speaks healing into broken hearts;
It speaks salvation into lost souls;
It speaks an end to all things wrong.

What word, Lord?
    Any word of Yours, I say, is glorious to hear!
And it has come to me so easily,
    on the backs of martyred saints,
        who heard the Spirit, and wrote.

I must thank them, one and all,
    for listening and recording
        this greatest of gifts—

The Word of the Lord.

The Gift of the Storm

The storm raged through the big bluffs of the winding, country road. The car moved at a crawl, practically stopped in the blinding rain—inching along the precarious edges of the mountain road, far from any house or even other traffic. The car rocked from the force of the swirling gusts. It was terrifying to the ten-year old child who sat in the front seat, between her aunt and uncle. She had experiences with weather that made her very prone to a fear of *any* weather, much less weather of this magnitude. Uncle Tom clearly struggled to control the car; the child was paralyzed with fear.

The faithful dog, Spot, lay on the floor of the passenger side of the car, near the feet of Aunt Eunice. His ears were showing some alert signs, but still he sat quietly and watched his master and mistress. They were as God to him, and their perpetual calm soothed him. All Spot ever asked was to be with these adored ones; nothing else mattered. But the child was not calm, though she tried hard. There were too many panicky experiences in her background—from parents who focused intently and fearfully on the weather.

At the signs of gathering storms—or even a heavy spring rain—her family had usually taken shelter in the local hospital, only a few miles from their home. How many days and nights had they dashed out—into the rain and elements—racing toward the shelter of the hospital! They had spent many nights sitting on hard plastic chairs in the lobby and gazing out to see if a funnel cloud might be forming, or if the wind seemed too high. No funnel cloud ever appeared, but even wind gusts would drive them farther into the innards of the hospital. The next refuge would be down the stairs to an underground basement, where you could no longer see the fury of the weather—and where they could only hope that the hospital would not collapse upon its refugees. (That possibility was mentioned often.)

In addition to this, her very early life in another place had involved frightening trips into an underground storm pit—filled with bugs, spiders, talk of possible snakes, and also rank, mildewed smells of earth—underground at its worst. And then there was the daily talk, talk, talk of weather—the stories of horrendous tornadoes, the aftermath of which the parents had witnessed, but not directly. There was also the time when a large tree actually blew down beside their house, scraping a side wall with a great scratching noise. This incident the child had witnessed herself and was greatly impressed with the force that could do such a thing.

So now, in this worst-case scenario, her fear spilled over into frantic crying. They would probably be blown over one of the steep bluffs, and killed. She knew the car was not the shelter they needed for a storm such as this. She would never see her parents and her brother again—and she was terrified to be in such a dilemma. She cried uncontrollably.

But Uncle Tom and Aunt Eunice were of a different temperament from her parents. They were not high-anxiety sorts. They were her dearly beloved second parents in so many ways—and such a contrast to her life at home that it was almost confusing to her, but always a pleasant retreat. She had never heard either of them raise their voices, either in anger or fear. Their lives were like a sea of calm, a seamless routine of peaceful duties and quiet conversation, of easy smiles and laughter, of simple pleasures and total acceptance. Their home, their presence, was a haven for beleaguered children—nieces and nephews who were eagerly welcomed by this couple who had no children of their own. And this particular child was convinced that she was the favorite of all the nieces and nephews. They were so eager to see her, so cheerful, so encouraging. She could feel their love from the top of her head to the tips of her toes. And their calm had always soothed her like a warm blanket.

And what happened to this aunt-uncle temperament in a *real* storm, a threat that was more than just imagination, a situation from which there was no refuge—no shelter in *this* storm—a situation where life could *actually* be endangered? Well, it was in this challenge that the child saw the reason for the consistent demeanor of her aunt and uncle; and she saw no difference in them amid the threat of the storm than in an ordinary day at their home. But it was their words in this crisis that turned her child's mind to a different place, never to return to the unbridled fear of that afternoon storm.

Uncle Tom told his niece that he was being as careful as he could and that he believed the storm would soon pass. But Aunt Eunice gave away the "secret" to their peace. She hugged the child and said, "We're going to be all right. If we get through the storm, we will be thankful. If this is the time that the Lord chooses to take us home to heaven, we will be even better. And me, you, Uncle Tom, and Spot will all get to go together!"

The little girl's mind released something that day. A great weight was gone; a thousand fear-laced conversations and flights to safety took flight themselves, never to return. Cured.

Wouldn't the psychiatrists and psychologists of the world be amazed? And to what should we attribute this miracle cure? Maybe it was this: The little girl heard truth—and she believed it. She had seen their truth in the ordinary times, and now she saw it in the jaws of death. They told her no lies, gave her no false hope, kept no secrets because she was a child. They told her the truth, the ultimate truth—and it set her free.

For to me to live is Christ, and to die is gain.(Philippians 1:21)

Good Friday—Now and Then

Good Friday today. Good for whom? Not for Jesus.

I recall another Good Friday when I was fifteen years old. I was a junior in high school, and the day had begun bright and sunny. Around midmorning, the sky became noticeably darker—and it seemed to happen rather suddenly. Within a fairly short time, the sky grew darker than any of us had ever seen during the daytime. We could not see anything but blackness in the sky—just as if it were night. No further attention to schoolwork was possible, either by the teacher or the students. We all actually felt rather terrified. All of us were mindful of the day. We all knew what happened as Christ was crucified: the earth turned dark on that original Good Friday.

An announcement came over the intercom from the principal. He told us to leave all our belongings behind, move immediately into the hallways, and listen for further instructions. Each hallway group was then directed, one by one, to move into the basement, the existence of which we students hadn't known up to that point. The basement consisted of a boiler room, pipes, and the machinery which apparently heated the school. Like sardines in a can, we were crammed into the bowels of the building.

We waited in virtual silence and a great deal of fear—expecting some unknown calamity, and sensing the reverence that must have stricken those who witnessed the crucifixion, as they also had watched the world darken in the middle of the afternoon. What could this mean? And could it be a coincidence that this was happening on Good Friday? As we later shared with one another, our thoughts had been pretty much the same. We considered that God might have chosen this most auspicious day to come back in His Glory, as a contrast to the Day in which He was so wounded, so undone—for our sakes.

But His return was not to be on that day, for the clouds lifted, and we returned to our routine. Nevertheless, this particular Good Friday would be etched in our memories forever.

Now, fifty-two years later, my mind still holds a vivid picture of the fury with which the elements revolted as the Son of God died for my sins.

The Terrifying Silence

We have known some little quiet,
some moments less noisy—
    But never silence.

The early morning may provide a fresh calm—
    dewy, muffled sounds—
but the birds speak their various languages,
and if a breeze comes, it whispers slightly.
Quieter moments these—
    but never silence.

A blanket of stillness falls
    over the watches of the night;
less sound needed in darkness,
    with bodies compelled to rest.
Sound reduced to lesser murmurs
    of night creatures in raw outdoors,
    or utilities running inside abodes of man—
        sound diminished—
        but never silence.

Our best quiet, always anticipating noise,
    so that even in sleep,
        no great distance exists
            between quieter place and sudden alarm.
For the quietest times of our race
    are subject to sharp intrusion—
        sudden blares, noisy crises,
        clamoring howls of life and death,
        the din of war,
        the sounds of harm—

lessened noise as we sleep—
but never silence.

But what of death?
Will silence come
        when clanking earth recedes?
Ah, but then the sounds
        of heaven or hell—
                unparalleled joy,
                or shrieking despair;
                        increase of sound—
                but never silence.

Until The Time.
The Time
        When He who formed us—
                Who allowed us to choose rebellion,
                Who watched our carnage,
                Who saw every injustice,
                Who heard every cry for salvation,
                        and let rebellion play its full hand—
                When *He* has deemed us done—

In the terrifying moments before
        He calls forth The Day—
                of full repay,
                of righting the Earth Ship
                        of every evil,
                        of every injustice,
                                from greatest to smallest,
                                from Eden to present.

And just before wrath yet unseen
        is about to be seen,
Come a few moments—

So solemn,
So terrifying,
So profound,
That unparalleled Silence
falls over heaven.

All the Hosts of God,
all the saints of the ages, arrived at Home,
hold their breath—
In reverence,
In stunned anticipation,
In holy fear
of the wrath of the Humble Lamb,
once offering eternal life—
now Judge of all the earth.

Unknown, unheard before—Silence.

The King is coming!
The King is coming!
Let all the earth be silent before Him.

When the Lamb opened the seventh seal, there was **silence** in heaven for about half an hour. [2] Then I saw the seven angels who stand before God, and seven trumpets were given to them. [3] And another angel came and stood at the altar with a golden censer, and he was given much incense to offer with the prayers of all the saints on the golden altar before the throne, [4] and the smoke of the incense, with the prayers of the saints, rose before God from the hand of the angel. [5] Then the angel took the censer and filled it with fire from the altar and threw it on the earth, and there were peals of thunder, rumblings, flashes of lightning, and an earthquake. (Revelation 8:1–4)   [Emphasis is mine.]

An Altered Fairy Tale

A well-known woman who led Bible studies for women once told of a brief encounter she had with another woman in her study. The second woman made the statement that she loved to think of the familiar fairy tale of Cinderella, because it seemed to symbolize the love and mercy that Jesus has shown to us as He pulls us out of the despair of our life situations—healing us, restoring us, and making us His own. Cinderella, the beautiful and kind stepsister, was rescued by a prince, thereby receiving a great reward for her long suffering. Likewise, the woman stated, we believers are Cinderella, and the Prince is Jesus.

The Bible teacher, upon hearing this analogy, strangely felt that something was amiss in this comparison but could not immediately identify what it was that did not seem right. She continued to think about this later, even as she was driving home. Suddenly she saw exactly what the problem was! In this classic fairy tale, Cinderella is a good and upright person suffering an unjust fate. She deserved to be rescued by the prince and to "live happily ever after."

The analogy completely breaks down for us, because none of us are good and upright, even the best of us. We do not deserve to "live happily ever after." We deserve hell as we stand uncovered as sinners in the face of God's Holy Being.

The true analogy for us in this story is that we are the ugly stepsisters. We do not deserve to go to the ball; we do not deserve to be rescued by the prince. Nevertheless, in this real and greatest of all stories, the Prince—Jesus—comes for us, ugly and unclean as we are. He comes for us before we are even dressed for the ball. He loves us with an everlasting love. He makes us holy and pure and beautiful, totally without any deserving on our part, and He rescues us from death and hell at tremendous cost to Himself. We go with our Bridegroom to the wedding feast prepared for us, and we live happily ever after.

Now *that* is a story to remember!

Must I Repeat Myself?

Out of the heart come the words—
delivered from the superior to the inferior.
"I've told you a dozen times …"

Really? That many?
Well, I can only say this:
    I asked you again because I did not remember,
        but you are so annoyed by my faltering,
        and *you* would never have forgotten, would you?

    Not yet. But wait.

And when the day comes that you must ask again,
    this is my prayer for you:

May someone whose tongue has been baptized in Christ's humility
    gently repeat again what you need to know,
        and not diminish you in any way.

I say this because I love you,
and I am also a sinner like you,
    a sinner who has injured others as well.

I don't condemn you;
    just asking for a little grace,
        and praying that humility will become your covering—
        and mine.

[AUTHOR'S NOTE: *This poem is based on an unkindness overheard.*]

Learning More than Literature

$\mathcal{T}$he college literature class was a favorite of mine. I determined to give it my best effort the spring semester of my sophomore year. The problem was that it seemed impossible to stay alert (and sometimes awake) during the eight o'clock class—even though morning had always been my best time of day. Try as I might, I would invariably end up with closed eyes, and one hand cupping my forehead so as not to be disrespectful to the professor. I sat in the back row and angled myself behind a large male student. My guess is that only those on either side of me recognized that I was not totally conscious during part of most classes.

My struggle on these mornings was not lack of interest or even lack of discipline. It was simply a story of over commitment, something I had no idea what to do about at this particular time. I was working so much that my study time came late at night, after I arrived home at about eleven o'clock. My workload was not an option, since at this particular time my family had to have my income in order to pay the bills, for we had fallen on hard times, with my father's poor health preventing him from working and my mother having taken a drastic pay cut at her job. Looking back, I suppose that an option would have been to not take any college classes, but somehow that made me fear I would be a college dropout. Consequently, I just determined to grin and bear it through this period, believing it would not last for a protracted time.

Basically, I stayed up most nights, studying until about three or four in the morning, and then rolling out for my eight o'clock classes. Even youth cannot sustain this for long, and my efforts to remain alert in class were growing more and more difficult. As for the studying, however, *that* I did—no matter what. I pored over every assignment, leaving nothing undone that I knew how to do. Therefore, my grades remained very high, and that was a major goal for me.

There is probably only one reason that I still remember this very mundane scenario: I learned an extremely important lesson that I have never forgotten—and one that has had thousands of applications over these many years. Therefore, I consider it a teaching from the Lord—a real living reminder to me of an important biblical principle.

My whole behavior pattern was different in this particular class, because I was normally one who eagerly participated in discussions and interacted with both the professor and the students around me. Like my father, I liked everyone, almost without exception, and had a natural friendliness and ease with people. But in this case, I came in and took my seat, with just a weak smile to my peers on either side; I then sat down and began the struggle to stay awake. I had little or no interaction with anyone, but it was not personal to them and entirely the result of my desperate lack of sleep.

I was to be jolted by the judgment of the girl who sat next to me in the back row. One morning, the professor was returning a major test to us, and our grades were written boldly on the front of the paper. She did not spare those who did less well by turning the paper facedown. So my test lay bare for my neighbor to see the score of 98, and some complimentary comments as well—all in red ink. As I reached for my paper, I heard a sneer coming from my peer. I instinctively turned the paper over, feeling almost embarrassed for some reason I did not understand. I heard her say something to the person on the other side of her, which I could not totally make out, but I did hear the snippet of "not even awake." I could not fathom why this should bother her, but I did not dwell on it. Later, however, the attitude was to be paired with something she had apparently said to a friend of mine.

A few days later, after classes had ended, my best friend on campus said, "I've got to tell you something you will not believe. You will die laughing!" She continued in a spirit of total merriment and said, "I know a girl in your Lit class who says you are the biggest snob she has ever met!"

"*What?*" I was incredulous.

"I know," said my friend, still laughing. "I told her, 'Listen girl, you have got the wrong person! She is a friend of mine and is the friendliest person I've ever known. She never looks down on anyone, never meets a stranger; you are way off on this one!'"

I immediately put this information together with the sneer from a few days prior and guessed the likely source of this opinion. To say that I was stunned is an understatement. There were many genuine flaws that a person could have rightfully pronounced against me, but in my heart of hearts, I knew snobbery was not one of them. Nor could I think of anything I would less prefer to be called than a snob—unless it was a thief or murderer.

I spent a lot of time trying to think how this could have happened. Slowly, I began to put together some explanation to myself. In that class, I did not interact with people as I normally would have done. A smile or simple nod was about the extent of it for those next to me. Secondly, my behavior of being only semiconscious every day probably conveyed the attitude that I considered the class boring or simplistic, that it was really beneath me. And this was further supported by my high grades, which probably said, "I can do this stuff in my sleep, while the rest of you have to study."

Yes, I think I put it together all right, and it made sense to me in this light. I was an affront to the girl next to me, without having the slightest idea how this was coming across. So what was the lesson I learned from this simple tale? Simply this: *Do not ever assume I know the contents of other people's hearts—their motivations, their feelings, the reasons for their behavior.* For this is God's realm alone, and furthermore, none of us can even fully understand our own hearts. Only He, our Creator, has this information. And He clearly has directed us to stay out of His business as He deals with each of us as precious "ones," unique of circumstance, and badly in need of grace.

Thank You, Lord, for using this small situation to teach me such a large lesson. I have not always obeyed this lesson, but it has ever been before me, showing me a slice of my own heart. I only wish I could go back and extend friendly and encouraging words to this girl who judged me so; for who knows what hurt and anger she was fighting at that time. I would like to have another chance to set aside my exhaustion and look about me to really *see* a person, instead of just extending a glance, for a glance is not really seeing. And continue to help me, Lord, to never think I know the heart of anyone, to never assume the worst of that person, to never cast him or her down in my own eyes. Let me forgive easily when judgment is placed against me. You alone, O Lord, are the All-Seeing God, the Judge of the human heart.

Two Women Died Yesterday

*Y*esterday, two women died. One was very old. She lived righteously for many long years; she had loved and served God for as long as anyone could remember. She did not have an easy life. Her only child, a daughter, was severely handicapped from birth, and she stood with and cared for this daughter in every way she could until the very end of her own life. She had lost her husband many years before her own death, and she and her daughter loved and looked out for one another for the years they were given together.

God was merciful, and this woman virtually died on her feet, with her good mind intact and at a good old age. She was a woman of goodwill and good cheer, a woman whose life was submitted to her Creator, whose trust was altogether in Him so that, even in the great difficulties of her life, she had a sense of joy and contentment. It was a life well lived, a testimony to the power of God and the blessings of obedience. She left behind her beloved daughter, who also knows and loves Christ, and will someday follow her mother to paradise. *This older woman now stands in the very Presence of her Lord, and surely the trials of this life are as nothing to her.*

On the same day that this righteous mother died, another woman also died. She was a young woman, also a mother, and still in her thirties. She had lived unrighteously for as long as anyone could remember. She was addicted to drugs and lived a promiscuous life before her daughters. She neglected her children, putting herself first and creating an atmosphere of chaos and carnage in her home. Her life was a nightmare filled with the reaping of her sins. She was found to have lung cancer at this early age, and began the grueling process of dying in the midst of her addictions and hopelessness.

But the same God who loved and cared for the older righteous woman also loved and cared for the younger unrighteous one. So in a series of very unlikely circumstances, He called on one of His servants, a teacher of the woman's daughter, to be drawn into the horrendous life of this family. An opportunity was given and taken to speak to this sin-bound woman about the true and living God who *alone* could free her from herself. When the young mother heard the very good news that Jesus Christ would forgive her, she repented with many tears. She had no time to learn to live out a long righteous life, and the few weeks left of her life were filled with pain and difficulty. She did not understand many things, but, no doubt, she had heard and answered the call of Christ unto salvation.

A few days before this young woman died, she managed to get to a church for a single time; there she worshipped and basked in the comfort of a song about heaven—that just "happened" to be planned on that day of worship. The very good news she had received with many tears was confirmed to her, and she greatly rejoiced. A few days later, she died. In her last hours, even when she could no longer speak, three young women, including the one who led her to follow Christ, quietly prayed around her bedside and spoke the truth of God's word in her hearing. She responded with a single tear of acknowledgment and joy. *This woman now stands in the very presence of her Lord, and surely the trials of this life are as nothing to her.*

> "For the kingdom of heaven is like a master of a house who went out in the morning to hire laborers for his vineyard. After agreeing with the laborers for a denarius a day, he sent them into his vineyard. And going out about the third hour he saw others standing idle in the

market place; and to them he said, 'You go into the vineyard too, and whatever is right I will give you.' So they went. Going out again about the sixth hour and the ninth hour, he did the same. And about the eleventh hour he went out and found others standing; and he said to them, 'Why do you stand here idle all day?' They said to him, 'Because no one has hired us.' He said to them, 'You go into the vineyard too.' And when evening came, the owner of the vineyard said to his steward, Call the laborers and pay them their wages, beginning with the last, up to the first.' And when those hired about the eleventh hour came, each of them received a denarius. Now when the first came, they thought they would receive more; but each of them also received a denarius. And on receiving it they grumbled at the householder, saying, 'These last worked only one hour, and you have made them equal to us who have borne the burden of the day and the scorching heat.' But he replied to one of them, 'Friend, I am doing you no wrong; did you not agree with me for a denarius? Take what belongs to you, and go; I choose to give to this last as I give to you. Am I not allowed to do what I choose with what belongs to me? Or do you begrudge my generosity?' So the last will be first, and the first last." (Matthew 20:1–16)

Disregard the Contrast

I see this young one,
    not fully reached manhood;
He sits in the aisle in God's sanctuary,
    in his wheelchair—
        limbs not cooperating,
        unable to stand,
        hands bent back,
        head slumped forward,
        unable to look ahead,
        gazing at his lap.

His voice sounds out in praise,
    not clear in words,
        but clear in intent,
            a sound of exuberant joy offered to heaven!

Here I sit in my pew,
    in a seat without wheels,
    able to stand,
    with hands that hold a Bible,
    with a distinct voice,
    with head held upright,
    with eyes that see ahead.

How shall I regard this contrast
    as I silently grieve for this one
        whose trials I cannot fathom?

I will regard it as You said, my God,
    that man looks on the outer form,
        but You see the depths of the heart.

Now, Lord, as You regard this heart
   of the one whose flesh is so shattered,
      You hear the praise from him that I also hear;
      and You see the life
         that will be lived so different from mine.

Would You grant me, O Lord, that I should be
   at least as grateful for my advantaged life
      as he is for his incredibly difficult one?

Or is it he, in his broken frame,
    the one who is more advantaged?
   Will he lean harder,
   Will he love more,
   Will he trust You
   at levels I may never understand?

And when the curtain falls
   on this realm of trouble,
      and when it rises in eternity—
when the broken bodies and hearts
   of the faithful are healed—
may we then understand how You molded us,
   one by one, in these individual calls,
      custom lives, made for the best good of each,
      all given as a gift from our Creator—

Won't we then see the lack of contrasts?
Won't we all say, "How He loved us all!"

And this one whose burden is so heavy here,
   will indeed stand,
   will have perfected limbs and voice,
   will lift his head and eyes
      to look into the face of Jesus.

The Tithe

It was my first year of teaching, my first year of having a professional job. I was sharing an apartment with a roommate who taught at the same school, and money was very tight, even with two of us splitting the costs. Teaching jobs were not a living wage at this time in the 1960s, so every penny seemed to count.

I was not very mature in my Christian walk at this time and did not fully understand the concept of tithing. My idea was more along the lines of giving the church a contribution here and there when I thought I could spare the money. I don't remember what caused me to come under conviction about this issue, but I was suddenly faced with the belief that I needed to honor God with at least a 10 percent tithe and be as generous beyond that as I possibly could. The problem was that every cent of my income was literally committed to bills and living expenses. In order to tithe, I would have to come up with an additional forty dollars each month (which clarifies the paltry income I earned at that time). I could not figure out any way that I could scrape up this amount.

After a considerable struggle, I decided to take a leap of faith and tithe on my next check, even if I had no idea how this would work out. This meant, however, that I would not have money to buy the groceries for myself and my roommate by the end of the month. We traded off buying the food and cooking on alternate weeks, and it would be my turn for the groceries on the last week of the month. I could not see my way clear to do this; nevertheless, I was determined to move forward with my tithing plan.

In all honesty, I thought I might have to call my parents for a loan at the end of the month—something I had *never* done and would have been totally embarrassed to even consider, but it was my fallback plan in my lack of faith. Of course, I knew this could not be the plan every month, so I also decided that I would probably need to get an additional job, which would have created a significant problem, since, as a novice teacher, I could barely cope with the rigors of preparing lesson plans and grading papers for the thirty-two sixth-graders who were presently in my class.

The check for forty dollars went into the church offering plate the following Sunday—with certain dread, I might add. The month then proceeded along; I paid my bills and pinched pennies as usual. The dreaded last week of the month rolled in, and I was scheduled to grocery shop on the last Monday, following the last Sunday, of the month. I practically had my finger on the dial to phone home, and, in addition to the humiliation of asking my parents for a loan, would have to confess to my roommate that I would not have the money for groceries until later that week. We would need to make do with odds and ends and scraps.

Sweating bullets, you might say, was what I was doing when I went to church that last Sunday of the month. I considered it the day before my "execution" the following day. But an incredible thing happened *that very day.*

One of the deacons came up to me after church. He said, "Charlotte, I have a check for you."

"*What?!*" I must have fairly shouted.

"Yes," he said. "At our business meeting this past Wednesday, we voted to start paying you a small stipend for playing the piano for the church every Sunday. I know you volunteered to do this, but we would like to show our appreciation, and we made it retroactive for this past month."

He handed me the check, along with a big smile. Imagine what a leap my heart, and my faith, took when I saw the amount of the check: forty dollars!

On His Lap

My brother was thousands of miles from home—on the other side of the country. He had been separated from his family by a contract job, the only work he could get at the time, and he seldom got home, even over a period of many months.

During this difficult period, he also became ill and at last had to be admitted to the hospital. It was discovered that he had appendicitis and that his appendix had ruptured. The only thing that saved his life was the fact that, miraculously, the deadly poison of the appendix had emptied into a protective sac and had not distributed itself throughout his body.

My brother was alone in this crisis, for none of the family had time to come to his side before the medical issue was resolved. Even afterward, there was no money for the airfare to join him.

I fully intended to make the flight to see my brother, since I had access to standby flying privileges. I called him to say I was coming, and to let him know how distressed I was that he had faced this alone. I was in for another of the many lessons that I had learned from my brother over the years. He was eleven years older than me, and he had spoken to me about God from my earliest memory. He always spoke of God in very practical terms, causing Him to become very real in my mind. Somehow, his view of God was different, more personal—even more so than the teaching at church—during the period of my childhood.

When my brother talked about God, He seemed more present with us—and so very amazing.

The phone call was brief. He was still in the hospital. I let him know I was coming to stand with him—and he let me know that he did not want me to make the trip, which was more than three thousand miles. He assured me he was all right, but I told him I just could not bear for him to be by himself.

"Oh no, I am certainly *not* by myself," he insisted. He then launched into his most recent blessing. "You remember how we used to sit on Daddy's lap, and it was the safest place in the world?"

"Of course!"

"Well, the Lord has given me a picture of this. I have seen myself sitting on *His* lap, and it really *is* the safest place in the world. Our earthly fathers can only take us so far toward safety, for we are all children needing a lap. I have seen myself in the safety of the arms of Jesus, and I am not afraid. Please don't make this trip."

He had done it again. He brought Jesus from far away to very near. Thank You, Lord, for this brother of mine. Now, all these years later, I rest in the knowledge that he has laid down this physical barrier and is in Your real Presence. Perhaps he is on Your lap.

I Said, He Said ...

I said, "It's a dark night, Lord.
I'll be glad when the dark is gone forever."

He said, "Here is a silver path of light
I am sending over your bedcovers."

I said, "It is beautiful, Lord, this shining lantern
in the night; but I long for *no* night."

He said, "Your real night has been lifted already,
for you are Mine."

I said, "Yes, Lord, I carry the light of life You gave me, but sometimes
the shroud of darkness seems too near."

He said, "Walk closer. In Me, there is no darkness at all."

I said, "I will set my face like flint, Lord, and look at You instead of
the darkness."

He said, "Then your darkness will be gone forever."

[AUTHOR'S NOTE: *Written during recovery from cancer surgery, spring 2012.*]

Black Patent Leather Shoes

*D*addy loved black patent leather shoes—not for himself, but for his girls, Mother and me. I knew this early on in my childhood, and naturally, I also thought these shoes were totally beautiful. It was Daddy who often called my attention to beautiful things, most of which were not material.

The very first pair of Sunday shoes I remember were black patent leather, and, when I put them on, I was like Cinderella going to the ball (or Charlotte Ann going to church). These shoes would cause you to dance, yes, even on Sunday. They would cause you to parade around in front of an admiring and whistling father; they would set you above the ordinary day, and let you know how very special was the day called *Sunday*.

And so it was that this early pair of shoes did their duty. They hung on when I managed to climb a tree before they could be removed after church. They withstood rocks and gravel around the churchyard as I played with friends after church. They protected my toes when I bumped them into stairs and scraped them through narrow places where children's feet often go. In all these circumstances, my patent leather shoes still managed to shine through increasing scuffs and slashes. And although I did not notice, my mother took note that I needed some new shoes.

It was not a small thing to get new shoes. I never had more than two pairs of shoes at any given time—an "ever-day" pair and a Sunday pair. I got new shoes when the old ones no longer fit my feet, and, if that happened to take a long time, my mother slathered on the shoe polish lavishly, filling the crevices caused by overuse, until I at least looked as if someone cared about my appearance. But patent leather was different. We did not know of a polish for patent leather or any other means of covering scuffs and other shoe injuries on these shiny surfaces; therefore, my patents had fallen into a sad state of disrepair. So my parents plotted as to how they would afford some new ones, although the old ones still fit.

I was too young to wonder how they came up with the money for this extravagance, but I do know it was discussed many times before it happened. I don't remember the actual purchase, but I have a clear memory of seeing the new, shiny patents being taken carefully out of the shoe box in my parents' bedroom. The new shoes were admired greatly by all of us and considered a tremendous blessing. I didn't realize that my old shoes were so awful until I saw the beautiful, unscathed new ones. Wow!

I was given some dire warnings by my mother about what *not* to do with these new shoes. Basically, I was to walk a straight path from our house to the car and from the car into the church. There would be no walking on grass or gravel, and certainly *no* climbing trees. I would be carried up the stairs if that was what it would take to avoid banging my toes on the steps. (I was not a careful child and would probably have been labeled *hyperactive* if anyone had ever heard the term in those days.)

And so it was that I put on my new shoes the following Sunday and marched into church, absolutely certain that every head was turning to admire these blazing new patents. This was preceded, of course, by much whistling and joyful approval by Daddy before we left home. It had even included a Daddy-daughter jig in the living room; for, after all, new shoes felt a special urge to dance—according to my father, who often assigned feelings and motives to inanimate objects.

Now this story could have well faded into obscurity and never have made the recall list of memories, since I was still very young when the event occurred. But the new patent leather shoes became attached to another event that was probably the real memory maker. This event happened soon after I got the new shoes.

Mother and Daddy had been talking about something that was more serious than usual. They spoke in low tones and left me with a sense that there were secrets about. After speaking this way for a while, they were ready to share the secrets with me. I sat on Daddy's lap, and they began to tell me about another little girl, just the size and age of me. I did not know this little girl, they said, because she lived in another part of town where people were really poor. They drew the contrast between our family and the family of this little girl. We were so blessed that we were even able to buy a pair of shoes before the old ones were outgrown. We sold some eggs our chickens laid and Daddy worked harder and we managed to pull off this amazing feat. But the little girl of whom they spoke did not have such possibilities. I don't recall the details of her sad life, but I was stricken to the heart when they told me her story. I had not heard of such things and had no concept of what to do, so I just cried, no doubt picking up on the sadness of my parents as well.

Then I was lifted up to hear that we would do something for this little girl and her family. Oh, how wonderful! Mother and Daddy said they were going to help; we were *all* going to help, even my brother and me. This was what Jesus did all the time: He loved poor people and helped them wherever He went. We would do this too, they said. Mother and Daddy were giving some of their clothes to the mother and daddy of this little girl. They were giving them some food too, and I don't remember what else. Maybe Daddy helped this father to get a job (I saw this happen a lot as I grew older). We were going to do all that we could—that was what I understood.

Now for my part. I do not recall being told what I should do. They just gave me a fact that startled my child brain. This little girl, they said, did not have *any* shoes. It was summer, and most children in the South went barefoot in those days—except to go to church. They wore shoes to church—*if they had any*. But this little girl had no shoes at all, and she had never in her life had any *new* shoes. In the past, the only shoes she had were ones that someone had almost worn out before she got them. She had never had any *pretty* shoes, certainly not any *beautiful* shoes like my black patent leather ones.

So you can guess the conclusion that was needed in this scenario. I had *two* pairs of Sunday shoes, and this child had *none*. She *never* had new, shiny, unscuffed shoes. I had some new, shiny, unscuffed shoes that she could have—for the very first time in her life. She could wear them to church, and I would still be able to wear shoes to church also. Amazing! There were two pairs of shoes and two little girls. Just what was needed.

Now I must give my parents a lot of credit for bringing me to such a place—a place where I could *hardly wait* for my unknown friend to have my newest and best patent leather shoes, while I kept the old, beat-up ones. I wish I could hear their pitch with my adult ears now. I'm sure the practical benefits were mentioned: you can resume the tree climbing and gravel kicking and you can walk up the stairs by yourself. And from Daddy, there was surely the mention that these old shoes had been somewhat sad to be replaced by shiny new ones—they would be so glad to be on my feet again!

But what I do remember is this: *Jesus will be pleased with this.* This is what *He* would do. He would give the best to others and keep the worst for Himself. Years later, when I read for myself the scripture which says, "In humility count others more significant than yourselves" (Philippians 2:3), I knew that my parents had shown me how this works. Thank you, Mother and Daddy, for casting this early vision for me in this real-life setting—and on countless other occasions during my childhood.

O God of Everything

God of Everything,
    God of me—

Remove from me
    any evil force
        that sets itself up against You;
        that binds my spirit to earth
        rather than heaven.

Call my mind and my spirit
    upward from this place as I pray,
        and set me before Your throne;
        that I may fall down
        with the Elders,
        and worship—
        without the claw of the enemy
        dragging me earthward.

Let all that I am
    in mind, body, and spirit—
        every cell,
        every corner of mind,
        the total of spirit within me—
worship You today.

As one whom his mother comforts,
so will I comfort you; (Isaiah 66:13)

Thelma and John: A Good Ending

$\mathcal{T}$helma and John were very old. They lived alone in a very modest house and had very modest means to sustain them. There were no relatives to care for them as they aged into greater and greater need. There were some social services available, but John and Thelma had a singular hope which kept them from asking for help: *they wanted to remain together as long as both of them were living.* Their fear was that in asking for assistance, they would be parted by well-meaning agencies; so they soldiered along, faring less and less well as time passed.

These two had once attended a local church but had quietly disappeared from the fellowship years before, apparently as a result of their declining health. This did not go unnoticed initially, but over time, their ties to the church seemed to be severed as those of their own age group died out, and new people came who did not know them. So they lived quietly but still with an active faith in God. Indeed, they were trusting God to take care of them and see them Home safely.

Somehow, a Sunday school class in their former church found their names still on a roll somewhere, but no one could recall who they were or what had happened to them. After finding their address, an inquiry visit was made to discover who they were and how they were faring. The visitor then reported to the Sunday school class that the needs of this couple were significant, but their hope of remaining together had stopped their seeking assistance. The class members felt a great deal of remorse upon learning this, as they realized that this couple had simply slipped under the radar of the church. They immediately made plans to act, and, ultimately, it became a story that played out just as it should when the Lord's people act like the Lord's people.

The first order of the day was to become friends with Thelma and John, and to pay them the respect that they deserved. The class members began to visit in groups of two and three. They began to discuss with these new friends how they could help in ways that were in keeping with the goal of remaining together. John, who was no longer able to walk without significant danger to both Thelma and himself, had the greatest need of the two. Also, his feet had sores which needed treatment right away. Thelma was very weak from trying valiantly to care for the two of them, and it was clear that they were not getting enough nutrition. Their house was in need of cleaning, since they were not able to vacuum and dust. They had no clothes dryer, and Thelma expended all her energy trying to wash and hang up their clothes to dry on a line in the garage. Amazingly, she still drove, and would venture to the store to buy the food and other essential items they needed.

Crews of new friends from the church began to show up to help with various projects. Early priorities were arrangements for medical help and proper nutrition. People brought food, supplementing this with a plan for Meals-on-Wheels to deliver daily. The house was cleaned and organized slowly, with respect for the wishes of John and Thelma. A great deal of material was sorted through, with much reminiscing on their part. A garage sale was held to bring in a little money, and many other things were donated to charity. Nothing was done without the full consent of the elderly couple.

Other social services were arranged, including home-care nurses who would help with bathing and personal hygiene, along with keeping an eye on the couple's medical needs. A dryer was purchased by means of donations from the church, and additional donations went toward purchasing other items which would simplify Thelma's daily tasks.

Real bonds of friendship developed, and the home of John and Thelma was often a beehive of social activity. At any given time, someone might be mowing the lawn, someone else preparing a meal in the kitchen, and still another person playing a hand organ and singing hymns with the tearful Thelma and John, who had not been with other Christians for a very long time. The elderly pair and their newfound friends shared their life stories, and the struggles and courage of this dear couple began to emerge.

It seemed that Thelma and John were the parents of one child, a little girl named Mildred, whom they loved dearly. But at age nine, the child had died, and they were left with tremendous grief. It was a heartrending story; however, the sound of victory was also heard, even in this tragedy, because Thelma was already a Christian when this happened, and John later turned his life over to Christ as well. Thelma said she thought at first that she would not be able to endure this trial. But as she and John walked into the funeral home where their little daughter was lying in state and as they were on their way to view the coffin, a gentle hand rested on Thelma's shoulder. She turned to see who was comforting her but no person was anywhere close to her. She whispered, a "thank You," under her breath, for she knew it was the Lord. She testified that she knew then she would be all right from that point on; for He would be with her always.

Yes, Thelma was all right. And so was John. They had a staunchness about them, a steadiness that came from confidence in God. They did not whine about things; they did not ask why things were so hard; they bore up under their assignments, and trusted God in everything. And then God provided a whole pack of friends who loved John and Thelma for as long as they lived—most of these people were the age that their daughter would have been if she had lived. Two of the members of the Sunday school class assumed guardianship for their care—with the agreement of John and Thelma, of course. And everyone saw in these two guardians the testimony of how the saints of God are to care for their own; and everyone saw in John and Thelma the testimony of how to grow old.

Eventually, the end came. John died first, in the hospital, but after only a day's separation from his Thelma. Thelma rejoiced that he had gone first and did not have to be alone. She would rather bear that burden herself. She rejoiced that they had gotten to stay together until the end. She rejoiced that she had so many friends. She lived in her home for some time after John had gone to heaven, and then wisely decided that it was too much for her. She asked her guardians to help her find a suitable assisted living facility. This they did, and she also determined that she should no longer be driving—without coercion from anyone.

A pleasant place was found for Thelma, and her friends visited her there, always finding the same strength and grace in this elderly saint. She was very direct in her speech, and her forthrightness garnered trust from her friends and helpers. She prayed for all she knew, and it was a treat to visit her because she was not self-focused or self-absorbed. She wanted to know about the people who visited her. And she frequently had small gifts to give those who came, for she was a crafter, always knitting and assembling various little items. She generously gave little treasures of napkin holders and knitted pieces. She also painted pictures of landscapes, and even portraits, and all of these she liberally positioned around her little apartment.

At a certain point, Thelma began to tell her friends that they would be welcome to one of her pictures when she left this life. She asked them each to put their name on the back of the picture of their choice so that it would be theirs at the proper time. The future recipients, all touched by this treasured gesture from a beloved friend, gradually affixed their names to the pictures as requested. There then came the time when a certain friend from the church was visiting Thelma, and she told the friend she wished she had a picture to give her, but all her paintings were already assigned—except, of course, for the painting of her precious daughter, Mildred. No one had chosen this picture; nor did Thelma expect it to be chosen, for no one knew this child who had been dead for so many years—and of course, this painting was very personal, so there would be a natural hesitation in claiming it.

But this particular friend saw something very wistful in Thelma's speaking of the lone picture left unclaimed. So she said enthusiastically that she would be delighted to have the picture of Mildred if that would not be inappropriate for her to ask.

Thelma was obviously surprised and pleased. A certain relief came over her, but she was not a person to gush her gratitude. So in her characteristic matter-of-fact manner, she said, "Well, in that case, put your name on the back of the painting."

The deed was done, and Thelma's treasures were all assigned. Her life continued on, with the same sensible surrender to aging as always. Her guardians faithfully looked after her interests, and her friends faithfully visited, standing with her even as she declared that she needed more intense care and willingly moved to another part of the facility where she would spend her last days.

At last the day came when a package was delivered to one of Thelma's friends. It was the oil portrait of Mildred, along with a small box of Thelma's greatest treasures: a few precious memories of Mildred—a picture, a report card, a child's drawing, a Sunday school pin, a lace handkerchief. The friend was honored by these best of gifts. She smiled every time she thought of them, knowing that Thelma, John, and Mildred were rejoicing together at last. And on earth, the victory was celebrated of two elderly saints aging well, keeping the faith, and letting go of this life so gracefully, as God's people are called to do. As for the church who loved Thelma and John and stepped up to be their many children, they were the ones especially blessed, all knowing they had received far more than they had given.

It was a story that played out just as it should when the Lord's people act like the Lord's people.

Living Sanctuary

We are walking in with sorrows,
Rivers of despair—
     despair of relationships
     despair of evil culture
     despair of tragic events
     despair of global failure
       under the domain
         of the ruler of darkness.

Walking into Your sanctuary
     where Your saints are worshipping;
       still praising You,
       still filled with impossible joy
         with impossible hope
         with impossible peace—
All clearly possible.

And we are singing,
     "My chains are gone, I've been set free
     my God, my Savior has ransomed me. ..."

Ransomed, O Lord; it is true!
Free, O Lord; it is true!
True when we are together,
     true when we are alone.

And we are singing
     "All the weak find their strength
     at the sound of Your great name. ..."

Your strength, O Lord; it is true!
Your Great Name, O Lord; it is true!

And we are hearing again—
    Your grace alone has redeemed us;
we must not clutter this truth;
    for gleeful joy
        is our only reasonable response!

We will take this sanctuary out with us
    when we leave,
        for we have remembered truth—
Together.

Let Your Light Shine on Us

$\mathcal{I}$t was a college classroom; it was early morning, when students struggled to be awake, would rather have been in bed, and clung to their caffeine to remain conscious. Just an ordinary day in the academic world—except for a divine interruption in the routine.

The college was, by statement and intent, a Christian college whose goal and purpose was to honor the name of Jesus Christ and to equip the students entrusted to its care to reach for the highest academic standards. Above all, both faculty and students were committed to a deep and personal relationship with Christ, seeking to know Him better with each passing day. In this setting, the common practice by each professor was to begin class with a short teaching from scripture, followed by a prayer, submitting to God the teaching and learning that would occur in each individual class.

A certain professor looked over the class of familiar faces on this particular morning. Many of their stories were known by the professor, for personal relationships were common between faculty and students. The professor knew of hardships in these young lives that could hardly be imagined; but the Refiner's fire had molded so many of them into beautiful lives of sacrifice and service, with bitterness and anger averted and replaced by love and healing. The professor smiled at these treasured ones and prayed silently that the Word of God would refresh and renew them for this new day.

A teaching from the scripture began. It was from the Old Testament, describing Moses as he obediently took on the assignment from God to lead an entire nation of former slaves through a wilderness experience and deliver them safely to the land which God had designated to their forefathers, a land that He was returning back to them after an absence of four hundred years. The Bible teaching showed clearly the struggle Moses was having with his immature and sometimes idol-worshipping charges. It was an impossible job in human terms, and Moses fully recognized this. It was a job which required total dependence on God. Moses recognized this also. His response, therefore, was to cling to God, in humility and obedience. The scripture said of Moses, at the end of his life, that he was the meekest man on earth.

The strength of humility was an important part of this teaching, reminding both professor and students that when they come before God, they all must do so with nothing to offer but the acknowledgment of their sins, bending their knees before the One who alone could save them. The teaching said that they then would be ready to serve Him who created them, Who loved them with an everlasting love.

The teaching continued, showing the specific effect of Moses's relationship with God, as he had just spent forty days in a close encounter with the Holy One on Mount Sinai. The power and majesty of God was so manifest in that place that the people below were forbidden to even come near the mountain, but, rather, looked on at a distance as fire and smoke poured out over the sacred place, terrifying them all. But God was molding the humble Moses, revealing to him in ever greater ways the very nature of his Creator. It was this relationship which sustained Moses for a lifetime, which filled him with the power to lead, to do the job that otherwise would have been impossible.

After many days of drawing so near to God, Moses at last came down the mountain and back to his people. He was a man changed forever, and even his countenance clearly displayed the fact that he had been with God. The Bible describes his face as shining with a radiance so intense that no one could bear to look on him, for he was reflecting the holiness of God. He had to put a veil over his face for a period of time, until God's glory slowly faded; only then could the people finally look upon his face.

The professor concluded this teaching and began to pray:

> O Lord, we bow before You, our Great God, and ask that we may know You as Moses did. We thank You that You have drawn near to us through our Lord Jesus Christ, that You have shown us how we may know You as a friend and a Savior. We believe, O Lord, that as You said while You were walking among us, that without You we can do nothing. We submit—

Just then, something intense and electrifying began to happen. The professor stopped praying, unable to speak in the presence of the power in the room. There was silence; no words were possible. Drawing in a breath, the professor wondering if others felt this Presence among them. The faces of the students reflected the same stunned breathlessness. No one dared move before the holy Presence—until a song began to rise from the students, a song of worship.

A young woman quietly stood at her desk and began to sing this song— in a beautiful, rich voice, echoing the words of this praise—a song which was really a prayer: "Lord, let Your light, Light of Your face, Shine on us. ..."

The other students and the professor joined in the singing. Faces glowed, perhaps with just a touch of the Shekinah Glory which had fallen on Moses. Tears flowed down these young faces in response to the almost unbearable joy. God had come very near to them in a simple college classroom, and none of them would ever forget that day.

Come and Worship ... What If?

We have singing, we have instruments—
    sometimes loud and beating,
    sometimes soft and soothing.

We have lighting, we have shades of color—
    sometimes bright and flashing,
    sometimes soft and muted.

We have images on screen, we have symbols—
    sometimes wondrous scenes,
    sometimes words to consider.

We have exhortation, we have prayer—
    basic thanks, needs' petitions,
    calls to look up, to ask.

Come and worship—
    ambience is planned,
    aids to worship provided—
        lights, music, images, exhortations, prayers—
            all good things for the prepared heart.

But what if ...
    the music stops,
    the lighting fades out,
    the pictures go dark,
    the words stop,
    the prayers of others cease?

Then, in the silence,
    without benefit of sight and sound,

without the aids of man,
without the strength of others—
alone in His Presence—
can we worship?

Can we hear the Voice
which spoke the world into being?
Can we face the Overwhelming Power,
or the profound peace,
of our Eternal, Transcendent God—
He who is bidding us come,
to join heart to heart,
Creator to creation,
in the silence found nowhere else
and for the only real rest ever found?

He bids us—
come and worship.

Last Wisdom

The young woman sat at the bedside of the older woman. Her friend and mentor was gravely ill, barely conscious, and only hours from death. They had been friends for many years, serving together in the same church. The faithful older saint had been a teacher of the young woman, and had delighted in sharing her love for God with her young friend over the years.

The young woman sat quietly and read from her Bible. She did not think her friend was conscious, but realized at one point that she seemed slightly more alert. So she spoke cheerfully to her friend, assuring her she was by her side. After a time, the young woman heard the last words of wisdom she would ever hear from her friend.

Quietly, but with great effort, came the simple words to her young friend: "Don't falter."

The young woman is now the older saint and the one who has herself reached out to so many in the name of the Lord. She also is delighted to share her love of Jesus with all who come her way. She is grateful for the many saints who have gone ahead of her, who invested in her life through their faithful teaching and friendship to her. And always standing in her memory, even after so many years, this powerful last testimony of the elderly saint: "Don't falter."

The Rotten Blueberry

$\mathcal{M}$y friend had many years of life behind her. She had relinquished a great deal of her independence, and there were many difficulties with people she loved. These issues could have been a great weight on her, but, instead, they flowed into her life as prayer needs, which in turn flowed up to the Lord, with the faith that lifted the burden and trusted in Him to answer.

Among the most challenging changes to which she had now become accustomed was the loss of the right to drive and to move about doing the things she had always done to minister to others for the sake of Jesus. Her errands had been her mission field; in grocery stores, she made friends with strangers and sometimes prayed with them in the grocery aisles. Her visits to the sick and elderly were continual, and had brought cheer and hope to countless lives.

But never one to stop ministering, she now continued to work for the Lord from her room in the house of her son—through the sending of cheerful cards and through telephone ministry in which she prayed with those who needed encouragement. If anyone picked her up to partner in a visit to the elderly or the sick, she was joyfully on board to go forth. In all the trials and changes in her life, she continued to give thanks.

Yes, thanks and gratitude to God poured forth from this elderly saint. With every obstacle, she trusted and thanked Him. In every good thing around her, she saw His hand at work. Nothing was too small, too inconsequential, for her to send up her joyful praise to God and to testify to others of His goodness.

A great example of "nothing too small, too inconsequential" happened one day as a friend picked her up in order that they might visit the sick together. She got in the car, with a radiant glow. It was the usual thing that she had some story of God's blessing to her, but this time it struck her friend as to the true level of gratitude which lived in the heart of this dear one.

"You won't believe how good the Lord has been to me this morning!" she exclaimed as she got into the car. "This morning I was fixing my oatmeal, and I had a handful of blueberries to put in the cereal. I washed them, and was letting the water drip from them when one of the berries fell out of my hands. I was amazed to see that it was a completely rotten berry! I would never have seen it, for all the other ones were good, but the Lord separated the one bad one out for me!"

Lord, let me be more like this friend of mine! Let my eyes see Your goodness at this microscopic level of the ways You bless me. In everything, let me give thanks to You!

Store-Bought Link

$\mathcal{I}$ have a friend who has lived many years for the Lord, and I asked her to tell me a story from her life that was meaningful in her relationship with God. She shared the following story from around her thirteenth year:

Janet's family farmed for a living, and times were hard for them and many others in those days. They had finally saved up enough money to purchase some tracts of land of their own, and had moved to a different rural area, near a creek and in the general vicinity of a little country church.

As spring approached that year, there was no money for Janet to have clothes for the warmer weather. She was one of seven children, and the only girl. Her winter clothing was all she had, as the family was at the end of their means.

One of Janet's aunts heard of this situation, and in a short time, sent her a package containing three "store-bought" dresses. Janet was amazed at such an incredible gift. For one thing, hardly any girl or woman had store-bought dresses in those times—and to think she had *three* of them! Since she had something to wear, Janet then determined that she would go to the little country church nearby. She did, in fact, go to that church—a new church to her—and it was there that she learned to trust in Jesus as her Savior. Her aunt's generosity to Janet had been used by God as one of the links leading to her salvation.

If I am not a chain,
Then let me be a link—
Just a small word or deed
That counts for eternity.

The Harvest

The harvest! The Harvest!
Labors of planting gathered in,
celebration for those close to the land;
     vague recognition from others
         that food will be possible
         for another year.

The cycle of life—
from beginning of time;
returning each in its turn,
     seemingly endless.

The seasons revealing also
     the lives of men:

Spring:
     birth,
     youth,
     freshness;
     life renewed
         like the new seed sown in the ground.

Summer:
     more maturity,
     hardest work,
     responsibility,
     hand to the plow
         like the farmer who labors over his crops.

Autumn:
     relief at the end of labor,
     celebration,

reaping the sown,
hoping for rest
    like the thankful farmer,
    glad for the harvest.

Winter:
    testing of living seasons over;
    endurance in the cold;
    Death—
        labor is over, and there is rest for the farmer.

The endless cycle of life will end
    by the design of the One who
        brought all life into being.

Then another Harvest,
the Final One,
the reaping of the crops of God.

He who planted,
    who gave all for the crop of souls,
        gathers in the faithful,
        the weary, the waiting,
        those who have asked
        down the halls of time—
        "How long, O Lord?"

Tears wiped away—
Celebration!
Joy of joys!
Feasting with the Bridegroom.
Ending the seasons,
    ending the winter,
        the dreaded season of death—

    Forever.

A Friend Who Prayed

*W*hen I was a child, my parents had to work very hard to make a living, often holding two and three jobs each. In addition to teaching school, my mother sold various household products and cosmetics, and she often ranged far out into the country in order to visit customers. She would give demonstrations of her products at the home of someone in a small community, then travel home late into the night, down lonely country roads, sometimes through dark, mountain passes. More often than not, I was with her, since my father was working at one of his jobs.

In one of these small towns, there lived a humble, elderly black woman whom our family knew well, because her sister had cared for both my brother and me for many years while my mother taught school. Our families had worked together as a survival team. So dear little Hazel was a friend who often hosted mother's demonstrations and gathered in the people of this rural area to see her products—and really it was a community fellowship, a jovial time for women to gather and eat little treats and exchange stories. Mother loved being part of this circle of friendship. She gave out simple little prizes at these gatherings so that no woman went home empty-handed.

Among the many memories of these times, the most poignant was the relationship of Mother and Hazel. How they loved one another—in the midst of the segregated South. Mother gave Hazel products and sometimes shared what little money she had if she sensed that things were too stark for Hazel to get by. Hazel hosted these parties, and the ladies in the community purchased most of their household cleaners and goods from Mother. After the party ended, often late into the night, Mother would pack up her goods to head home, and then she and Hazel would have a few minutes to sit together as friends. Mother would be tired, no doubt dreading the long, dark trip home, especially with a young child in tow. Hazel always grew concerned about the lateness of the hour, haunted by the thought that our car might break down in a place so remote that we would not be rescued for many hours, or, perhaps that we would be involved in a wreck—as well as any number of other dangers we might encounter. So I can never forget the image, repeated so many times, of their last hugs good-bye, followed by Hazel slipping to her knees in front of her "praying chair."

"Miz Johnson," she would say from this position on her frail little knees, "I be right here before Jesus 'till I knows you be home safe. He will show me when to get up."

And so it was, over many trips, over many years, that Mother always arrived safely home. A better friend and a better gift could not have been had. Hazel was a lot older than Mother, and the Lord called her home first. How Mother wept when she heard of this earthly loss. But time is short for us all, and now the friends are spending eternity together—where there are no more dark roads, no more poverty, and no more segregation.

Help for Listening

Lord, I am calling out to You.
    Would You hear me, and speak back
      in Your own way?

      And this time, I want desperately to listen,
        but even in this endeavor, Your power is needed
          to overcome the flesh which wanders
            into its own fleshly zones,
            and tunes into the world and its issues,
            and takes counsel with self first—
            instead of You.

      Lord, I see that this monologue is not prayer—
        for prayer listens as well as speaks.

Thank You for this moment of truth,
    for this speaking into my mind;
it *is* a conversation, is it not?
Would I speak a monologue to any human,
      any friend, or even any acquaintance?

Would I not be quiet, and listen
    to the response of any other?
How much more shall I listen
    to the True and Living God?

So, speak, Lord; Your servant is listening.

He Visits the Humble

An elderly man was asked to pray at the closing meeting of a certain Christian conference. The man's hair was white with age. His back was bent, and he walked with the caution of age as he climbed the few steps to the podium to offer the prayer. He faced the audience with a radiance of face, clearly reflecting the Master he had served for so long.

The people at the meeting knew the story of this elderly saint and held him in high esteem because of his life of faithful service to his Lord. They knew he had served as a missionary in an Asian country for more than fifty years. Indeed, the reason he was asked to this particular occasion was because of his influence and witness to the man whose ministry supporters were meeting at this particular time. The man who headed the ministry was Asian by birth, and as a young man, the missionary had played a significant role in teaching him about Jesus. Now the younger man had an international ministry, and his mentor's efforts were bearing much fruit. Thus, he had invited the faithful saint to this conference in order to acknowledge and honor him.

The missionary's body bore the scars of his years of service in difficult places, but his spirit bore the imprint of the years of following Jesus. He stood before the group, holding the podium for steadiness, and then began to speak to his Lord in prayer. His words of humility were a plea to God, not an invocation to the audience. But the power of his words struck all the listeners as he lifted his voice to heaven, saying, "God, be merciful to me, a sinner!" (Luke 18:13).

The audience was pressed down where they stood, feeling the power of the unseen Presence. Many wept, and all worshipped. The Holy Spirit was among them that day, riding on the humility of God's old saint.

A Prayer for Our Shepherd ...

Lord, would You please bless this man
    who shepherds us,
    who exhorts us with Your powerful words,
    who calls us to righteousness,
       and reaches out to us in tenderness.

Would You please give him the spirit of Moses,
    that he may endure our grumblings,
    that he may intercede for us when we don't deserve it;
    that he may be sustained and comforted
      by Your call to continuing faithfulness,
      and by Your power in the face of all.

And, together, with our pastor,
    may we also be blessed
    by close encounters with You;
      and, together, may we come to know You
        at such a deep level
          that we may be called Your friends.

Lord, refresh our shepherd,
    so that he does not carry the boulder
    of our troubles—
    or even the boulder of his own;
      but give him the burden that is light,
      the yoke that is easy,
        that he may live joyfully in trial or in pleasure,
        and not dread our company,
        but be blessed by us,
          even as we are weak.

Would You please, O Lord, set Your words in his mouth,
 Your wisdom in his mind,
 Your rule over his heart,
  and arm him against the deceit of our times;
   so that he may boldly call us from
   the dangerous places
    where our enemy would lead us
    to be devoured.

Bless our shepherd's family, O Lord.
Bless the godly mate You have generously provided,
 the woman your Word describes in the Proverbs.
May she have an uncommon wisdom,
 singularly fixing her heart upon You.
And for the children You have given them,
 may each of them be blessed of God;
 may they each serve You faithfully all their days;
 may they each be as King David,
  servants after Your own heart.

And for us who are blessed by our pastor—
 would You call us to continual prayer for him,
  that Satan will not be able to sift him.

And let us not expect unreasonable things of him,
 or forget that he is a man, as we are.
Let us not cling to him instead of You,
 or behave as milk drinkers,
  rather than meat eaters.

But let us walk beside him,
 and take his counsel as from You.
Let us pour out our love on this servant
 whom You have sent us,
 by whom You have blessed us,

and through whom we are receiving the
  words of life—

The Lord be with him in his comings and goings,
  now and forevermore.

Joe and Margaret: Courageous Lives, Faithful Lives

*O*ne Sunday morning, an elderly couple came into a new Sunday school class. In fact, they were in a new church and a new denomination altogether. He was eighty-seven, and she was eighty-nine. They were not new in the area, no not by many years. Actually, they had come from a church in the same town, a church where he had served faithfully in many responsibilities for thirty years. Now they sat among strangers, confident that in their last years they would find new friends. They came in good cheer, with kind eyes and kind words, with expectations to serve rather than to be served. They had nothing bad to say about their former church, and it was a long time before anyone knew their reasoning for making such a difficult change. Finally, when some new friend was bold enough to inquire, they simply said, "We had to leave because the Word of God was no longer preached, the Bible no longer believed."

So, in their new fellowship, they continued to serve quietly but powerfully. She cooked for anyone who would come to her home, although her sight was so poor that her husband had to help her identify the foods to put together, had to help her set the table, had to help by being her eyes. Her great heart was totally unimpaired as she joyfully received all who would honor their home with a visit. She tried to anticipate every need, tried to exhibit every graciousness which would speak to her guests that she truly honored them, and all with the genuine humility of a servant serving someone greater than herself. How she spoke to us like that of one wearing the mantle of Christ Himself!

Though her eyes were dim, she still served, and with less-impaired ears, she listened to our stories, inquired of our lives, as we sat at her gracious table, feasting on her baked goods complemented by warm beverages. She never referred to herself except in an apology for some perceived weakness, some lack of ability to serve us better. But, one day, my husband and I determined to hear her story, and we pressed her to tell it to us. Though it took coaxing, an incredible story, a slice of her life, at last emerged. She obviously chose this recollection because it represented to her the mighty hand of God, who had spared her life and the lives of others in a desperate hour.

Margaret was born and raised in Germany, remaining there through her youth. She married an American and moved to the United States. At the time of the story she recounted, she was the mother of young children, and she had returned to Germany to visit her family, only to find herself unable to leave because of the impending collapse of the German government as World War II came to an end in Europe.

She was in the small village of her childhood, and American troops began advancing toward them. This was a dangerous situation for them, because a man from their village had just ambushed and killed an American soldier. The Americans were prepared to destroy the village and smoke out others who would not surrender, thinking this to be a stronghold of dissidents. The villagers, not understanding the American ethic of valuing life, believed that they also would all be brutally murdered as just retribution for the crime of one. Indeed, the village was in danger unless the Americans could be convinced that this was not a collective effort to kill their soldiers.

Only one among them could speak English, and that was Margaret. She elected herself as a party of one to go to the Americans and beg for the lives of the villagers. She set out on a lone journey to meet them before they could reach her family and neighbors, and, at last, she located the Americans. She was one desperate young woman facing the army of the enemy, there to beg for mercy, to beg for their lives, to apologize for the foolishness of one among them. She was a shy girl by nature. Now, she was terrified; she was unequipped—except for the hand of God to give her favor.

The Americans were merciful; their anger toward the village relented, all because of the earnest pleas of the young woman. They believed her, spared her friends and countrymen, and reached out to the village in kindness. This was one little slice of the story of Margaret and her part in history.

As for her husband, Joe, he immediately began to serve the Lord in his new church. He began a ministry to the sick and to shut-ins, visiting the hospital routinely and turning up wherever people were lonely and in pain; visiting people he did not know, encouraging them with his prayers and good cheer. He quickly gained the respect and admiration of his fellow believers in the new church. They trusted him and sought his counsel.

On one occasion, he delivered some of Margaret's famous chicken soup to a woman who had just had surgery. He stayed to talk for a few minutes, and upon inquiry about something in his past, he related a story that had been an important part of his life.

Joe had been married twice before his marriage to Margaret. In each case, he had been left a widower. His second wife was stricken with Alzheimer's disease, and Joe chose to retire early so that he could take care of her until the end of her life. The decline was many years in the making. Joe grew weary and prayed daily for strength to keep his commitment to his wife. On one particularly exhausting morning, a home-care care worker came in to check on his wife. Joe was in the process of feeding her, and she was having a hard time swallowing the food. As the worker observed the scene, she told Joe it was time to get a feeding tube, since it looked as if his wife could no longer eat by mouth without choking. The worker then left the room to get some supplies, but her words had stricken Joe to the very heart.

"No, not this, Lord!" he cried out! Somehow, it was unbearable to him that his wife should endure such affliction. "Please, Lord, don't require this of her!"

Joe's words were barely spoken when he saw her chin drop to her chest. She took a long, last breath and moved into eternity to meet the Lord whom she had loved. Joe began a praise of weeping that could hardly be contained. He saw the mercy of God as never before. Even as he retold the story after so many years, his tears of joy and thanksgiving were clearly evident.

After only two years of faithful service in their new church, Joe was diagnosed with leukemia and began to decline rapidly. He consented to chemotherapy simply because he wanted to remain as long as possible to care for his Margaret. However, he became so ill with the treatment that he saw it was not a good answer. He opted to stop the treatment and was told that he might last two or three weeks. He accepted this with the same calm and peace that he lived his life. He had already made every arrangement for Margaret that could be made to ensure her care in his absence. Her family would gladly care for her, and Joe was satisfied that he could do no more. He spoke to the church at a Wednesday night prayer service, telling all that he would soon be going home to be with the Lord. He thanked them for their kindness to him and to his Margaret. He bade them all a temporary farewell, and exhorted all to keep the faith and finish the race. It was obvious that Joe was a man without fear, knowing the Lord would soon take him Home.

True to the prediction of the doctors, Joe left this life within three weeks. After he was too weak to attend his beloved Sunday school class, but before he slipped into a coma, his friends in Christ gathered to record a video message for this treasured friend. One by one, they stood before the camera and spoke words of love and encouragement to Joe. They all knew the good-bye was very temporary, and they said so. It was as if all were going on a magnificent trip to the same place, and Joe was just going on ahead. They waved and smiled; they cried. "See you there, dear brother!"

The tape was shown to Joe. He was too weak to speak, but he smiled. *Yes, my friends, I will see you there!*

Lord, how I thank You for the testimony of the lives of these two dear saints. They have shown so many of us how to grow old in Christ, how to be of good cheer, how to work to the end of our days, and how to finish the race, with complete confidence in our future.

Return to the Light

For those of us who have despised our sins,
    have cast them into the River of Blood,
    have wept with relief from the burden unbearable,
    have been dressed in the perfection of Your life,
    and are not stranded in the blackness of our own hearts—
      You have not once failed to sustain us.

For You have given us the Pierced Hand to hold,
    and You will not release us, will not release *me,*
    though I will invite the dark fog again and again.
Even so, I see the Wounded Hand, holding me fast,
    even when the full light is obscured by my sin.
      But I immediately miss the light,
      and the darkness is intolerable!

So I come quickly to wash again and step back:
    into the cleanness of a fresh bath,
    into the light yoke, the easy burden,
    into the clarity of forgiveness,
      where my gaze can now follow upward
        to the Hand that holds me in the fog,
        and lets me see clearly again the Light of Your Face.

Let's Just Go!

A little-known story played itself out in a nursing home. It is the kind of story that Christians know is just the normal fare for those who follow Jesus. Nevertheless, it is a reminder of the great victory ahead for fellow travelers who are themselves bound for heaven; and it is perhaps a mystery to those who are not Christians.

This is the story of three people whose lives were linked first and foremost by their bond with Jesus Christ, forgiven through His payment on the cross for their sins. Second to this, they were linked by family ties. Their family ties can best be explained in relationship to a fourth person, with whom they were all connected. You see, these three people in a certain nursing home were, respectively, the husband, the mother, and the mother-in-law of another Christian, whom we shall call Julie.

Julie was standing in the midst of a severe trial as these three of her closest family members were seriously ill. Her husband was dying of cancer, her mother was dying of many old-age maladies, and her mother-in-law was suffering similarly. Her mother-in-law had some issues that affected her ability to speak her thoughts clearly, and her mother was blind. These two elderly women had a long friendship which they had maintained through their physical decline. When unable to visit each other in person, they spoke on the phone, encouraging each other in the Lord and often singing hymns together as they ended their conversation. Two of their favorite hymns were "No, Never Alone," and the old gospel song, "Come Home, Come Home, It's Suppertime."

Now these two friends were ending their days together in the same nursing facility, along with their son/son-in-law, whom they both loved dearly. They were wheeled around for common visits with one another as they were able. They often held hands and sang their songs of victory, as they understood that glorious days were soon to come to all of them. On one occasion, a family member witnessed the mother holding the hand of her son and saying, in her limited speech, "Let's just go now! Let's just go!" He agreed it would be a wonderful thing if they could "just go." She meant, of course, that it would be such a glorious experience to go together into their eternal home and be in the Presence of God—neither one would then have to grieve over even the temporary loss of the other.

Not long after this touching scene, the day came when the first of these three got the call Home. It was Julie's mother. Julie's sister was preparing to go for a visit, planning to help her mother eat her evening meal; but before she could leave home, the facility called to say that her mother was declining rapidly. Julie and her two sisters were able to quickly go to the side of their mother and stand with her as her soul was taken into heaven. They were able to sing songs to her that she loved, and they realized, as they sang "Come home, Come Home, It's Suppertime," that the Lord was actually calling her at the very time of that particular meal. How it made them smile at the thought of this! They recognized this special gift from the Lord, which added to their comfort. And this was not at all unusual, of course, for all their lives they had experienced an untold number of times when God had reached out to them and to other Christians in these very personal, direct, and meaningful ways— just to show His great love and care for them.

After a visit from the pastor, the daughters of this faithful servant of God sang a parting song to their mother: "This World Is Not My Home." They were blessed! And their mother was even more blessed, as she answered the call of her Lord to "come Home."

Within only a few days, Julie's husband was called to his heavenly home. His suffering was over, his new and incredible life was beginning.

Amazingly, within only a few more days, his mother also received that most important Call. And so it was that the three members of the same family (but, more significantly, members of God's family) were able to step into eternity within mere days of one another. What a reunion that must have been! Called from cancer, tumors, blindness, terrible suffering, and old age, to glorious healing and restoration—into the very Presence of their Savior. And if they found joy even in those days of tremendous trials, we can only imagine the joy they are sharing now!

And what of dear Julie, whose human losses were so great? She will not escape sadness, will not escape loneliness, and will shed tears for her temporary losses. But she knows the same "secret" that her loved ones knew. Her secret is Jesus Christ, the only hope of heaven, and the One who will sustain her all of her days—until He invites her also to join that great celebration for the redeemed.

Once Upon the MARTA—A Quick Assignment

$\mathcal{A}$ family crisis was going on in Florida, and I was living in North Carolina. I headed back to Florida again, one of several trips already made. The stress of the problems awaiting, the unsettled problems left behind, and the sheer tedium of travel all combined to cause great mental fatigue. I asked the Lord to give me the necessary physical and mental strength for the days ahead.

On this particular trip, I traveled in an odd combination of modes. I drove our car to Atlanta and left it with one of our daughters who lived there. She took me to the MARTA (Atlanta's rapid transit train) station, and I rode the train to the airport to catch the plane to Florida.

Weary to the bone by the time I got on the MARTA train, I began reading a book to pass the time and get my mind off of my troubles. The train stopped at each station, and was gradually filling up between the north side of Atlanta and the airport. Most seats were taken, but the one beside me was still empty. At a certain stop, a man boarded and headed toward the vacant seat next to me. I glanced briefly at him and acknowledged him with a nod. I saw just enough to know he was a man in trouble. He was a thin, frail-looking man who smelled of smoke and alcohol. He had a bruise under one eye. I returned to my reading without any further thought of the man. After all, I was overwhelmed with my own issues. But as I was settling into my book again, a jolting sentence blasted through my mind with startling clarity: "Tell him I am the answer to his problems."

That got my attention completely; it also frightened me. The "I" was immediately understood to be God. Was this really God speaking to me with an assignment, or was I hearing my own thoughts? It was totally odd and outside the realm of any experience I'd ever had; therefore, I was afraid to ignore it. I had a major adrenaline rush, sensing an urgency about the matter. Was I really supposed to deliver some message to this total stranger? I began frantically speaking with the Lord in my mind: *Lord, surely this is not from You! I don't even know how long I have to talk to this man or where he is getting off. Help! Is it You?*

Even as I inwardly uttered this prayer, the man himself provided the answer. He looked right at me and spoke with perfect clarity, words which made absolutely no sense for him to be telling me. He said, "I'm getting off at Five Points." And Five Points was, in fact, coming up fast. I was beyond astonished at this direct confirmation to my question. I had to quickly eliminate the mistaken thought that I could have a significant talk with this man. After all, that was not even the assignment. There was absolutely no time. *Obey, now!* The man was just about to get up as the train came to a halt. I only had time to say what I was told—no dialogue, no explanation, no getting acquainted.

I turned to the man and said,

"Sir, the Lord Jesus Christ has just spoken to me and asked me to give you a message. He wants me to tell you that He is the answer to all of your problems."

He stared at me, mouth open. The door had opened; he had to go. He got up, almost too slowly to get out. He stared at me, as if trying to grasp what I had said. I knew my words struck his heart, which he had heard and understood. He went for the door and exited the train. He turned back, facing me, standing outside the train a few feet from my big window, still staring, mouth open. The door was closing, and we were about to pull off—all so fast! We looked at one another in a profound moment of time. Slowly, the shadow of a smile broke out on his face. I smiled back at him and pointed toward heaven. The train was moving, but we both looked at one another for as long as we could. He waved to me. I waved back. I knew the Hound of Heaven was calling him.

"I hope to see you in heaven someday, brother," I whispered. My exhaustion fell away, replaced by exultation. *O Lord, in the midst of my troubles, You have given me an assignment and reminded me of what really matters!*

Brought to the Bridge

We thought the apple was good; we ate it,
  with a mere nod of perceived appeasement
    to The Only Good and Wise God,
  but still following our own thoughts,
    and careful to not move
      too dangerously close to the Spirit,
      where we would be transformed,
        really transformed,
      where we would find what it means
        to *walk* in the Spirit,
        to *worship* in spirit and in truth,
      where we would opt
        for the greater life over the lesser one,
        for the saved life over the damned one.

But in all this, Lord, You have pursued us
  through the long days and nights
    of our estrangement;
  through the lies
    of our false religions,
    our made-up gods.

You have loved us
  with an everlasting love
    that wishes none of us to perish;

You have known that some of us
  would finally listen and some would not.

You knew we would be in trouble;
You knew You would stand
      between us and the Dragon.

You knew some of us would come
      to the end of our own plans,
      would despise ourselves;
      would repent in dust and ashes,
          as did Your servant Job,
              and would at last be saved
                  from the enemy of our souls.

You built that priceless Bridge
      by which we can
          survive Your Presence,
          be filled with Your Radiance,
          be handed Your Righteousness—
the Bridge of Jesus the Christ.

We bow before You with thanksgiving!

The Inheritance

I once heard a story from a man I did not know. He told me his story with great enthusiasm, with tears coming to his eyes, and I listened with rapt attention.

My aunt and I were attending an old-fashioned gospel singing at a little country church. It was in the small, rural town where I had spent my earliest years. I knew some of the people, but my family had moved from this little town when I was very young, and I did not know the gentleman with whom I was speaking.

Aunt Eunice, also formerly from this area, would occasionally introduce me to someone, always explaining the association with my father, who was raised in this town and had once served as mayor.

"This is Sox Johnson's daughter," my aunt said to this particular man, whose name I cannot now recall.

Usually, this introduction produced a flurry of comments about my father and the good memories of his public service and love for the people in the area. Many said they remembered me as the little blond girl who was often seen tagging along with her daddy.

But, in this case, when the introduction was made, this man drew in his breath and said with reverence, "Well, then, you would be the granddaughter of Mrs. Beulah Doughty!"

I was pleased to acknowledge this kinship, as I loved my grandmother with all my heart.

The man then let me know that his life was linked with hers in a very important way, and he proceeded to tell me the story of their connection.

It seems that when he was just a young man, he was rebellious of heart and did not want anything to do with God. He knew my grandmother well in our small town, and she was especially fond of him. (I think everyone who knew her felt the same way—that she was especially fond of them, for indeed she was.) Apparently, my grandmother was aware of his spiritual condition, and, knowing her as I did, I feel certain that she had been praying for him. She also was never in the business of condemnation, for she loved saints and sinners alike.

He continued his story by saying that someone had pressured him into attending a revival in town, and he had been immediately sorry that he had come into a church. He was very uncomfortable in this setting, in which his way of life was set against the contrast of scripture's promise of *real* freedom in Christ. He did *not* want to give up his lifestyle, even though he had noticed that he was really quite miserable. And now he found himself under great conviction from the preaching. When the preacher invited all those to come forward who wished to submit their lives to Christ, be forgiven, and enter into a new life, the man found himself in a real inner struggle. He did not want to "give in" to this call.

In the Baptist Church in those days, you answered the call to salvation by a public action, which meant going to the altar and declaring to the preacher that the Holy Spirit had convicted you of your sins and that you wanted to surrender your life to Jesus Christ and be forgiven. But during the singing of the invitation chorus, the young man stood in his own pew and gripped the back of the pew in front of him. He was stubborn, he told me, and determined to not heed the call of God. He just needed to get out of there as soon as possible, but he was stuck in the middle of a row of people and could not leave without becoming a spectacle.

This was the point at which his life intersected with Grandmother. He saw a commotion to his left, and looked over to see Grandmother stepping over all the people on his row to get to him. She was holding out her hand to him.

It must have been quite a picture to see. Grandmother with silver hair, styled in the typical grandmother bun of braids, and rimless glasses that featured the kindest eyes you could ever imagine—eyes that always smiled and told all those in her gaze that she loved them. She was small in stature and somewhat bent over from the meningitis that had afflicted her as a child. She wore sensible, black, grandmother shoes that laced up, and she walked with a limp. She wore cheerful dresses with flowers, always adorned with a brooch. She cried easily, for her heart was very tender. And above all, she loved Jesus—as everyone who knew her could attest, for she *looked like* she loved Jesus.

"Your grandmother," the man told me, "was reaching for me. She had tears for me rolling down her cheeks. She told me to come on, she was going to the altar with me, and it was time for me to be saved. She took my hand, not caring what anyone thought—and all my resistance melted away."

"That was the day of my salvation," he continued, "and Miss Beulah's hand reaching to me was like the hand of Jesus. I have never been the same. She went to the altar with me. She cried, she prayed. I cried, I prayed. I surrendered to Jesus."

My precious grandmother had been with Jesus for many years when I met this man. His story reminded me what a sweet aroma of Christ she was to so many people. For me, the story was a gift—the reminder that I have received a rich inheritance, and so have my children and their children, and so have my nieces and nephews and their children. For her prayers were many for the generations that would follow her, and surely those prayers still stand before the throne of God, pleading that we will all find our way Home through the cross of Christ.

I will be ever so glad to see you again, Grandmother!

> Know therefore that the LORD your God is God,
> the faithful God who keeps covenant and steadfast love
> with those who love him and keep his commandments,
> to a thousand generations, (Deuteronomy 7:9)

Remembering the Incarnation

Our thanks to You, our Great God,
    for the returning season
        of Your Incarnation.

Still it stuns us, makes us stagger
    to think of its import.
For now we have life and not death;
    now we are people of hope;
    now we can rejoice
        above all happenstance.

Draw us now, O Lord,
    above the world's irreverent party,
        and into the quietness of soul,
            as we remember our Holy God—
        The once Christ child.

He Knows Your Name

$\mathcal{S}$ometimes God gives a sudden and urgent assignment to one of his servants. It may be totally unexpected and even shocking. An evangelist once shared his story of such an assignment.

The evangelist was holding a series of special revival services at a church in a small city. The power of God was clearly moving, night after night, as evidenced by an outbreak of confession and repentance among the people. Crowds were at the altar each night, weeping with both sorrow and relief as they received the healing power of the Holy Spirit. The prayers of the Lord's people filled the sanctuary.

On this night, the evangelist stood quietly and joyfully as the Spirit moved among the people praying at the altar. He glanced about to see if he might be used by the Lord to minister to any person. His eye caught sight of a young pregnant woman, bowed down and weeping bitterly.

At the very moment the evangelist caught sight of this woman, the Lord spoke to him with startling clarity: "Her name is Carolyn. Tell her that I love her."

"What, Lord? Is that You?" the evangelist asked.

"Call her by name."

The stunned evangelist moved toward the young woman. "Carolyn?" he inquired.

The young woman looked up. "Yes?" she said, through her tears. "How do you know me?"

"God told me your name. He told me to tell you that He loves you."

Great sobs came from the young woman. When she was finally able to speak, she said, "Oh, preacher, you don't know what I just told the Lord. My sins are so great, and I have strayed so far from God that I don't know how He can forgive me. I had just said to Him, 'Lord, I've been in such great sin. You probably don't even remember my name!'"

No Grace Is Given

No grace is given, no grace is given,
though much is given to me.
I scan the broad landscape, I peer into the corners
to see what I can see.

I see your mistakes, I see your sins,
how clear they are to me.
I pronounce my judgments, I state my conclusions,
what should and ought to be.

And as my tongue informs your ear,
This is what I *fail* to see:
I miss the light that leaves your eye
as I take your hope with me.

Had All You Can Stand? Maybe Not ...

$\mathcal{M}$y cousin was at the end of her rope. Her husband was seriously ill and in the hospital; furthermore, he was in an advanced stage of Alzheimer's disease, with the question of using a feeding tube (or not) looming near. She was exhausted from having cared for him for years, to the neglect of her own health, and stricken over the tragedy of spending the early years of what was to be their pleasant retirement watching her husband slowly disappear from her and from himself. She dragged herself to the hospital to see him on a particular morning, exhausted from little sleep and the continual responsibility before her. She got to the parking garage at the hospital and began to look for a parking spot. None was to be had.

"O God!" she cried out. "Please let me find a place to park—*close by.* I'm too tired to walk a long way."

Nothing. She drove around and around, finally crying as she continued to drive. It was one trial too many, even if it was only a small one.

"Just a close parking spot—can't I have that?"

No, you may not. But after several more tear-filled rounds, a vacancy came at last—about as far as possible from the entrance to the hospital.

Another story comes from a dear friend. It was many years ago, when her four children were young and needing maximum care. Her husband was working full-time in a Christian ministry, and his work was with teenagers. Many of them had serious problems—problems which continually landed in the arms of my friend and her husband, in their home. They seemed to have a steady flow of teens who needed a place to stay temporarily, who needed counsel, food, hope, love. To put it in brief terms, she was exhausted, mentally and physically, and with very good reason.

One morning, in desperation, she fell to her knees and cried out to God, "Lord, have mercy on me. I just can't take any more!"

While she was still praying, the doorbell rang. She got up and answered it, only to meet a young man who ended up staying with them for an extended period of time, and who turned out to be a sociopathic con artist, ultimately causing them endless trouble and confusion.

What are to be made of these stories? They come alongside all the incredible victory stories we often hear from the saints of the Lord— stories where things just work out miraculously. We all have heard— indeed we all know personally—the testimonies about God coming through just in the nick of time, of Him catching us just before we go over the edge, of His provision just when needed. But then there are also those instances when you are going down for the third time, but guess what—there's a sociopath at the door; there's no parking spot close by when you are too tired to walk. You can't take any more, but you *will indeed* take some more.

Job knew how this felt. Elijah knew. Joseph knew. And then the One who profoundly knew—Jesus, who bore the wretched unholiness of us all, Who desperately wished the cup could pass, but it didn't.

> who for the joy that was set before Him
> endured the cross, (Hebrews 12:2).

How shall we think about this? Is God punishing us? Is His wrath turning our way? Are we just reaping what we have sown? Is He testing us? Does He not care about our desperation? Are we just getting what we deserve? No one should be presumptuous enough to proffer an answer, but we *can* be bold enough to *eliminate* some answers by way of scripture.

Are we getting what we deserve? *Not possible. Our next breath would be taken from us.* The cross has prevented us from getting what we deserve. It also prevents the wrath of God from turning our way. His wrath has turned from us once and for all. And it once and for all answers the question, *Does God care?* There never has been, nor will there ever be, an answer about caring like the answer of the cross.

As to reaping and sowing, it is an immutable law, of course, but does it apply in the cases above? Maybe or maybe not. But on the surface, who could assign blame to either of these women for what happened to them?

As to testing, these were certainly trials by fire. And only God's own counsel can say if and when and why we are being tested. We only know with certainty that whatever the reason, *it ultimately will be an act of love, done for our benefit in ways we cannot yet know, and may never know in this life.* But we know with certainty of the power of our God to redeem *all* circumstances, even thwarting the evil of Satan himself—and turning it to be used for the glory of God.

These women were stretched beyond endurance—or so it seemed. But where are they now, years beyond these experiences? They are following Jesus without hesitation. They have grown stronger with passing trials—more committed, persevering, pressing on toward the prize. They both believed that they were at the end of what was humanly possible to endure. And they were probably both right. Yet, they endured. They endured because there was a Power behind their weakness. But at those moments, they didn't *feel* the sudden boost of power and encouragement that often surges with the Presence of the Holy Spirit. They felt alone and hopeless for a period of time.

But there is a promise made to us by God Himself which counters any feeling, any circumstance, and any hopelessness.

"I will never leave you nor forsake you." (Hebrews 13:5).

And in those dark moments when God seems to have retreated to some other place, we know that it is not so. But it is possible that He is moving out ahead of us, calling us to come deeper, to cling harder, to seek Him anew with all our hearts, because we cannot bear even a small distancing from Him. But all the while, whether or not we *feel* the hair-raising Presence, we *know* the Everlasting Arms of the Lord are beneath us, and our gift of faith will allow us to step into the darkness, knowing He will be there.

What Vehicle?

I am strife.
I have a voice of my own, a tone—
    pinched,
    bearing down against opposition,
    starting opposition,
    seeking superiority.
      Intense, self-defensive,
      easily offended,
      loud.

I do not give way—
    for I am right,
    always right,
    righter than you.

I have a greater message
    than the *issue* before us.
You should know this:
    I am superior to you.
    You are lacking.
    Your opinions are without worth,
      compared with mine.
    I am standing on principle,
      on absolute rightness;
    therefore, you must bow to right,
      for there is no compromise
        with right.

And *I* deliver this right message—
    In my shining vehicle of **pride**.

I am truth.
I have a voice of my own, a tone—
>   clear,
>   open throat,
>   not talking over,
>   hearing you,
>   respecting differences,
>   not taking personal offense,
>   gentle—
always about conversation,
never about argument.

I am also right, and
>   there is no compromise with right.
But not right
>   with my own rightness.
And I do not defend self.
I have no issue apart from truth.
But truth without love is not
>   complete.
So I hope your spirit
>   will hear my tone of love—
>   in general—
>   and in particular for *you.*

I hope you will come with me;
I hope I can call you
>   to the only truth that matters.
I hope I can introduce you to
The Way, The Truth, and The Life.

May the vehicle of **humility** call you.

The Mary Stories
Part 1: But There's Mary

"*It's* a friendly neighborhood." The woman who sold us our town house proceeded to elaborate on the various neighbors. And then, just as a contrast to what she had said, she added, "But there's Mary, two doors down; she just keeps to herself."

I hardly know why I remembered this comment, since my husband and I were leading such a busy life that we had no thought of getting to know any neighbors beyond just making their acquaintance. We had just retired, and then moved, almost in the same breath, and were taking on significant responsibilities with a Christian ministry in our new area. My husband was working full-time for this ministry, and I was a volunteer with the same ministry—not to mention the myriad of issues afoot in our families.

Nevertheless, God has His own agenda and His own timing—if we have ears to hear His assignments. I'm afraid that I didn't have a good history of being still and listening, but, rather, of jumping up and getting started—with my own plan, which I tended to assume was approved by God. I was about to have everything I knew about obeying God altered forever.

It was several weeks after our move; we were settling in. It was a quiet day of husband at work and wife cleaning house. I was running the vacuum cleaner—with no particular issues at the forefront of my mind.

A voice interrupted my normal thoughts. It was an inner voice, but certainly not mine: "Go see Mary."

"Mary who?" I inquired aloud, startled by the words I'd just heard.

"Mary who lives two doors down."

I immediately recalled the only other information I had about her, the words of the woman who had sold us our new home: "But there's Mary, two doors down; she just keeps to herself."

I was so stunned by this abrupt deviation from anything I had been thinking up to that moment. It then occurred to me that this was likely a message from the Lord. It had an urgent feel about it. *Don't even finish vacuuming. Just go.* I turned off the vacuum cleaner and headed out, wondering what on earth I would say when I arrived two doors down.

I knocked on the door and had almost decided to turn around and leave because there was no response in a reasonable length of time. But then the door opened—somewhat, that is; maybe twelve inches. A head appeared, with the body still safely behind the door. The woman was older than me, with grayish hair, and beautiful but not-so-trusting eyes. She looked tired and sad. She waited for me to speak.

I introduced myself as her neighbor, two doors down. I said I had not been very neighborly since we moved in, but now I just wanted to introduce myself and let her know that I did not work except to volunteer, that I would be around some during the day, and I hoped that perhaps she would come and have coffee with me some time soon. I gave her my most enthusiastic invitation, very genuine, for I was touched by the great sadness I saw in her.

She thanked me without much life in her speech, and made some comment to the effect that she did not get out much to visit. I said I would certainly be glad for a friend in the neighborhood and hoped she would call me soon and let me put on a pot of coffee for us. I gave her my phone number. She never came from behind the door and just looked all the more uncomfortable as I spoke. I thought it best to not press further and just gave her a warm good-bye, saying I was glad to meet her.

Now, since I assumed this was an assignment from God, considering the unlikely possibility that I could have thought this up on my own, I fully expected that Mary would just think this over for a few days—maybe even just one day—and pop right on down. In my enthusiasm, I was totally convinced that we should become great friends. Well, that was not the case. Days passed, then weeks, and no Mary.

This could not have been an assignment from God, I told myself. *I was just having odd thoughts and attributing them to God.*

So the incident fell off my radar, almost forgotten—until another vacuuming incident occurred. Same thing, exactly. Same startling voice, same instructions. I was beginning to be afraid this time. I was afraid I was getting delusional, particularly because this in no way felt like my own thoughts, and I dared not ignore the emphatic instructions. I was also afraid because I had no idea what I would say to Mary *a second time.* How was I supposed to strong-arm her into having coffee with me?

Don't finish vacuuming. Just go.

The urgent pressing won, and out I went to knock on Mary's door again, having no idea what I would say a second time.

This time, the door opened very quickly and very wide. It was not Mary, but a large older man who looked neither friendly nor unfriendly. I was totally startled by this and asked if Mary was home. He said she was not, but he would be glad to give her a message. I introduced myself and told him I would really like to get to know Mary, since we were both home during the day and I thought we could be friends. He actually looked pleased at this and said he would definitely deliver the message. I thanked him and left.

Again, I expected fast action. After all, when I received the message, it was urgent—as in, *go right now, without delay!* But, once again, days passed, and nothing. I was greatly doubting that God had told me to do this, and I was confused, wondering how and why I could have come up with these emphatic words to myself. I told God all these things and asked Him to help me not to be so fast to jump to conclusions. Plus, Mary was not even home on my second visit.

As this second incident also began to fade into the background of life's other issues, a most unexpected happening occurred. It was during a workday, but my husband, Bill, just happened to be home, meeting with some service workers. I was away on errands. It was at this time that Mary actually chose to come to our house. Later, she told me that she was stricken with guilt when her husband told her that I had returned to invite her over a *second* time. He must have had some influence on her also and made the invitation seem more legitimate. At any rate, Mary decided that she must do the decent thing and come tell me something important so that I would not continue to call on her. The important message was that she was just not the neighborly sort, and although she appreciated my kind efforts, I should not pursue this further.

She had her speech ready—for me—but not for my husband. So when she arrived at the front door and Bill answered it, she was totally taken aback, and this threw her off her plan altogether. She tried to give him the message, but he started telling her how glad I would be that she had come. He stepped outside onto the little front stoop to talk to her and insisted that she come back again when I was home. Something went awry with Mary's words, and instead of delivering her intended message, she began to tell Bill that it was not a very friendly neighborhood. She then launched into a list of her troubles—the words exploded from her, so many and so serious that it was Bill's turn to be overwhelmed.

He had no idea what to say to her or how to comfort her—except for the obvious comfort that any Christian can offer to anyone in trouble.

And that is precisely what Bill did: He told her that he could see how serious her troubles were, obviously beyond the ability of mere humans to solve. He told her he knew the only One who could help and asked her if she knew the Lord Jesus Christ. She said she sort of did, but it was obvious to Bill that she did not understand what a real relationship with Christ was all about. Bill then said he wanted to pray for her. He put his arm around her shoulders and began to ask the Lord to hear his prayers, and to reveal Himself to Mary and to help her. Mary broke into tears, crying through the whole prayer. Bill insisted again that she should return and visit with me. She finally thanked him and stumbled back to her own place, obviously shaken.

Amazingly, Mary turned up at our house again; the very next day, if I recall correctly. This time I was the one at home and enthusiastically invited her in. Her intention was still to give me her brief message of refusal, although she was still shaken from the power of Bill's prayer the day before. She did, in fact, give me her planned speech, stating that she was just not the neighborly type, but she very much appreciated my kindness in reaching out to her in friendship, especially the *second* time. (Yes, it was the second visit that clinched it!) Nevertheless, she said, she was pretty much a loner, especially when it came to being friends with women. The simple reason for this, she told me, was that she constantly compared herself to other women, and always ended up feeling inferior. She gave me an example to explain what she meant.

"This house is entirely too neat," she told me. "My house will never look like this, and I can't even relate to someone who can do this."

I was astonished at this generalization, because, at any given moment, my rooms might look very different, but I could see that she would not believe any protest I made. Then I had an incredible thought! We were living in a three-level town house, and the bottom level (which was our office) was an area that I simply could *not* get under control. It was a wreck; everything I did not know what to do with or have a place for I left there, pending further thinking about what to do with it.

So I said to Mary, "Well, you have caught me on an odd day, or you would not see such order around here. But just come with me, and I will show you the *real* me."

I led her down the stairs to the basement where I presented the chaos. With a proud wave of my arm, I said, "This is the real me, Mary. I bet you can't top this!"

Mary surveyed the wreckage, and I sensed her increased admiration for me. "Well, all right," she said. "Maybe we *can* be friends!"

Subsequently, I repeated the invitation for a cup of coffee, and she decided to visit with me for a while.

The next few minutes were life changing for me. Mary gave me my next "test" by sharing an overview of her very overwhelming life. The words tumbled out, and she looked at my face for signs of horror and rejection. She had been married five times and had four sons, each by a different father. She was an alcoholic, not presently drinking, but not sure sobriety would last, since she had previously gone years without drawing a sober breath. Her eldest son was a heroin addict, and her other sons also had big problems. It was all her fault, she said, as she had been a terrible mother, and she never had a moment without torture of conscience. She had been a prostitute at times in her life. Her husband was ill and probably dying. Her childhood had been a nightmare of the worst order, with parents who hated and rejected her and her siblings in every way possible. Her siblings were as messed up as she was, and her brother had spent most of his life in prison. She was bipolar, and on and off of medicine—mostly off. She had been an avowed atheist since the age of seventeen, but she had recently begun to think that she should investigate God again, though she generally blamed Him for her terrible life.

After Mary finished the unveiling of her tragic life, she sat quietly, looking at me for some reaction. I was stricken to the heart and fighting back tears. She then gave me a sad look and said, "So you see, how can you and I have anything in common? You obviously have a great life, and I am a total mess."

I don't remember exactly what I said to Mary then, but I did let her know that we *could* be friends and that I was so very sorry for the things that had happened in her life. I also told her I knew for sure that things could be a lot better. I told her I was a Christian and that the Lord was the only hope for me—or any of us. I told her I had indeed not had a perfect life and that I was a great sinner just like everyone else.

She then told me that she had been back to the very formal church, the faith in which she was raised, but she found no answers there. And she said she had also gone to some "weird" groups, as she called them; the description of which told me they were New Age organizations. She had pretty much rejected these groups because she said they sat around talking about how they were all going to be "gods." Mary's exact comment in regard to this was "If I am a god, we are all in trouble!"

As we said good-bye, I told Mary that the important thing was for us all to find out who God really is, and then I suggested that maybe she and I could search out the scriptures together to find answers. I asked her to come back, and she said she would.

The door closed behind Mary, and I collapsed on the floor in a desperate cry to God. I had no idea what to do, how to deal with this precious, wounded woman—neither what to say nor where to start. Not a glimmer of a plan came to my mind. I had no skills, no experience, no thought as to what could be done. I told the Lord how helpless I felt, not knowing how to deal with this situation and not understanding how to even manage the first step. I could not imagine that He would choose someone so unqualified to take on Mary. But I learned that God could choose anyone for any task, for God plus anyone is sufficient. I also learned that I should never again assume that I was capable of running with my own plan.

This first encounter with Mary changed my perspective forever. I learned what it really meant to trust God for every move, and I understood what Jesus meant when He said, "Without me, you can do nothing." A long journey of discipleship and friendship was to follow, and the Lord brought many others to join this road leading to Mary's salvation. *I stood in awe* of what God did in the life of Mary, how He astonished us both with His very specific and tender care of her. *I stood in awe* of the ways He revealed Himself and showed His unconditional love for a poor, beleaguered woman who believed that she was unworthy of the regard of anyone, let alone God. *I stood in awe* that God would allow me to witness a transformation as complete as that of the unsaved Mary to the saved Mary. Surely, no one was ever loved by God more than Mary. And just as surely, none of us is loved less.

The Mary Stories
Part 2: Introduction to Church

*M*ary went to church with us for the first time. She had not been to church in years, and never to a more informal church like ours. She *wanted* to go because she was at last seeking to know God. Yet she did *not* want to go because of all the many preconceived notions she carried with her:

- she was not worthy because of her sinful life;
- she would somehow be exposed;
- people would know she did not belong there;
- she would feel inferior to everyone there, because they were good people and she was not;
- she would not know what was going on;
- they would be teaching from the Bible, and she would not understand it.

As we walked down an aisle to our seats, Mary muttered aloud, "Here's ol' Mary McMurphy goin' into a Baptist church. I can't believe it!"

We took our seats: Mary and I sitting beside each other, and my husband sitting on my other side. God was there to meet Mary that day. The interim pastor, older and wiser, was handpicked for Mary. He stepped up to the podium, the lights above him shining on his peaceful face. It was a face molded by the many years he had followed Jesus, and it reflected the character of his Master. He told us all that we had come to an appointment to be with Jesus that morning, the One who would be receiving us just as we were and looking to forgive our sins and take our burdens from us as we worshipped Him.

This opening invitation of love and welcome was too much for Mary, whose life was filled with untold misery, sin, and guilt. She broke down immediately and began to weep. She clearly felt the powerful Presence of the Holy Spirit, and she could not understand what was happening. She struggled to regain her composure but was touched throughout the entire service by a power she had not previously known.

As the pastor invited us to open our Bibles so that we might begin the study of God's word, Mary nervously muttered something about how she would now be found wanting. The truth was that Mary had never in her life had contact with the Bible until the week prior to this particular Sunday. We had sat at my kitchen table and had coffee together as we opened the Bible to the Gospel of Matthew. This was the place where I had decided to begin teaching my friend the Word of God. We had covered only the first chapter during the entire week, because of all the riches and background that came into the teaching, even in a chapter concerned with a great deal of genealogy. Therefore, this first chapter of Matthew was the sum total of what Mary knew about the Bible. And now, sitting in church with people she believed were much nicer than she and whom she supposed were all filled with a vast knowledge of the Bible, Mary was completely intimidated. She hung her head in shame, believing she would be noticed and exposed for who she was.

The pastor opened his Bible and invited us to follow him in the teaching of the day. "Open your Bibles to the first chapter of Matthew," he announced.

Mary shot a stunned look at me. "You arranged this!" she whispered.

"No, Mary, it was not I who arranged it. It was God."

For the second time that morning, Mary wept uncontrollably—and I have to admit, so did I. It was one of countless times when I was privileged to see how much God loved Mary.

The Mary Stories
Part 3: Testing the Waters

$\mathcal{M}$ary and I became friends very quickly, once she discovered that I had imperfections; however, for a long time, one of her recurring themes was that I was morally superior to her. It took years to dislodge this idea from her mind, and only then was she able to see me as a struggling sinner just like herself. This process began as she gradually accepted the fact that God really loved *her*, in spite of her sins, and also, as she came to understand that *none* of us are good compared to our holy and perfect God.

Mary was hungry for truth. We studied the scripture together morning after morning. She began going to church with Bill and me on a more regular basis. Others began coming alongside of her as friends and mentors. Mary was very intense and very unstable in her moods. She could wear a person down pretty quickly; however, before any of us were totally overwhelmed, another would step up and share the work that God was doing in Mary. This sharing the load just seemed to happen; it was not a planned hand-off, for lack of a better term, but just seamlessly came about as needed. It was an amazing thing to see the Lord Himself do the planning and scheduling, to give each of us the words to say, to mentor dear Mary in such powerful ways and with the involvement of so many people. And it was amazing to see the specific ways He did personal things for her that could not have been merely coincidental.

However, in spite of these many occurrences, Mary was very resistant at times, often coming close to surrendering to Christ but then throwing out a test of sorts for some of us, as if we were the ones to be examined instead of the claims of the Lord. She would alternately have a show of faith and trust, and then retreat into disbelief and anger. She made several alleged professions of faith which were clearly not the real surrender. During these ups and downs, which were very taxing on those around her, the Lord brought enough people to walk with her that none of us reached a point beyond endurance. Many others had a story of Mary during this period, but there are two that I recall from my husband's and my experience.

Mary was raised with a Catholic background but had raised her fist to God when she was seventeen years old, telling Him she did not believe He existed. This was an illogical act, of course, to talk to the One whom she did not believe existed. Clearly, she *did* believe He existed, but she was letting Him know she was angry—and, furthermore, that she was going her own way from then on. Of course, her "own way" ultimately led to a shipwrecked life in every way possible. But then Mary had lately begun to think that maybe she could "check out God" again. One of the many routes she took was to slip in and out of the Catholic Church. When she and I began our Bible study together, I told Mary that although I was in a Baptist church, I was all for any denomination that taught the Bible faithfully, believing it to be the inerrant Word of God. I was not trying to convert her to become a Baptist; I was trusting God to call her to be a *Christian*.

As mentioned, ultimately, Mary went regularly to church with my husband and me, but not before she put me to one of her tests. She thought it would be fun to invite a Baptist to a Catholic church, eager to watch me squirm with discomfort because it would be so different from my church. I did not worry about "squirming" with the form of worship, but I was concerned that familiar traditions might distract her from scripture, and I knew Mary needed to focus on the truth of scripture. The Lord impressed upon me, however, that I was to go with her and that He would show me what to do.

My trip with Mary to this Catholic church turned out not to be a regular Catholic Mass, during which I might have been a little confused as to how to respond appropriately. It seemed that Mary had come across a group of charismatic Catholics who invited her to a nighttime meeting. Having studied Catholicism for years, it was probably true that I understood Mary's religion better than she did, even in the traditional Catholic Church. But she certainly had no concept of *charismatic*. And I had no concept of *charismatic Catholic*. So it was that we turned up at a nighttime meeting of a group of charismatic Catholics. It was an experience that neither of us would forget.

In the first place, the scripture was read and taught. That night, it was a passage from Ezekiel in which God raised up the "dry bones." The teacher said that he feared for churches where the Word of God was not taught to the people, and that in those churches, the people were like the dead bones, needing life restored to them by a relationship with Jesus. *I was stunned!* Next, someone shared a prophetic word of a vision received from God. *Mary was stunned!* After that, they began a period of active worship, with singing, lifting hands in praise, sometimes dancing before the Lord, and praying—all at the same time. I was really tracking with this group and joined in without hesitation, having a wonderful time indeed! Mary was in shock. When it was over, I felt that I had a whole new group of friends, but Mary was practically dragging me out of there.

"What a bunch of crazies!" she couldn't wait to tell me. "What was happening in there, and how is it that you, a Protestant, fit in, and I felt like some trespasser?"

"Well, I told you, Mary that I can worship with anyone who believes and teaches the Word of God in truth, and that is exactly what they did."

Mary said some other things, not fit to repeat, but as for me, I was completely marveling that God would turn Mary's testing back on her and prove the truth of what I had told her. However, that was Mary's last trip to that church.

"We better stick with your church," she said. "They can stay calm." I had a good private laugh at this assessment, realizing that Mary was just trying to avoid the conviction of the Holy Spirit that she had felt with the charismatic Catholics.

Another example of her testing us came one Sunday after church, when Mary was having lunch with Bill and me. Mary was making provocative statements, loudly expressing her doubts about God, and throwing out challenges. It was clearly not about sincere questions and concerns, but, rather, about her anger. She often gained satisfaction from upsetting others.

In the midst of all this provocation, Bill shocked me almost senseless by suggesting to Mary that she should read Jonathan Edwards's sermon "Sinners in the Hands of an Angry God." I tried to nudge him under the table as he gave her a brief idea of what this writing contained. I was absolutely certain that Mary was not ready for such a work as this, in which Edwards compares sinners to a spider dangling treacherously over the pit of flaming hell, held only by the merciful hand of God and ready to be cut loose in an instant. All this is described in the most vivid and terrifying manner in Edwards's treatise. I believed that this reading might set Mary back irreparably—but my husband continued to give her a little sample of the sermon.

Mary was astonished at these thoughts and said she would like to read this sermon. So the moment we arrived home, Bill got our copy of Edwards's sermon and took it right to her. I was really stressed over this, but too late!

Well, as it turned out, "too late" was not the correct sentiment. "Just in time" would have been better. Mary called me later that day and asked to come over. When she arrived, she was clutching the book in her hand and she could hardly wait to tell me that she had been stricken with fear over the reality of hell. She said she realized she had been fooling around too long and that she had better "get serious" about God. After that, the testing pretty much ended.

Not long after this event, Mary truly surrendered her life to Jesus Christ. This time, we all knew it was the real thing. She was examined by the pastor at our church, and she prayed the saving prayer, in which she asked to be forgiven of her sins and placed all her hope and trust in God's Son to save her for all eternity. She asked to be baptized as a believer, and soon it was done. She was so thrilled to show publicly that she was a follower of Jesus. This woman who once hid behind her front door to keep from being noticed was now boldly proclaiming before hundreds of people that she had become a follower of Jesus. She told us afterward that as she was coming up out of the waters of baptism, she could almost hear Handel's "Hallelujah Chorus" being sung by the angels!

The Mary Stories
Part 4: Restoring the Years

$\mathcal{M}$ary and I spent many mornings at my kitchen table, looking out of the large windows onto a deck where the greenery of spring and summer and the myriad of birds drew attention to the hand of our Creator. And in the winter days, when the frost lay heavy on the ground and the trees were bare, we held warm cups of coffee and thanked God that we were warm ourselves—and blessed with a friendship in which we could share the best and worst of our lives.

Mary's background was so filled with horror that it had beaten her up for her whole life. Her parents were cruel and rejecting, leaving Mary with a sense of shame that she had been unable to overcome. It left her hiding in the shadows, afraid to approach people as someone worthy to be seen and heard. She wanted to be invisible. The only format she had found for interaction with others was in Alcoholics Anonymous, where she could tell her stories over and over and go through the Twelve Steps endlessly. And, while it is true that she was no longer drinking, she was anything but free. She would go from group to group, always looking for new ears to hear her stories—hoping that somehow she would begin to feel better about herself if she told these things to enough people. We began to see this pattern as an unintended crutch for her, though a great deal had obviously been achieved by her attachment to AA, since she had been sober for a significant period of time. Now she was using them to call attention to herself and trying to heal by telling her stories ad nauseam. She was stuck.

After Mary began to surrender her life to Christ, she gradually began to be *truly* healed. She sat at the kitchen table many days and wept and wept out the hurt of the years, mostly as she studied the Bible and began to see God's love for her. She continued her habits of going from meeting to meeting for a while after she began her relationship with Jesus, but the need began to fall away, and, ultimately, she had no need whatsoever to revisit the past and torture herself endlessly about what had been. Instead, her focus came to rest on the person of Christ and the pursuit of a daily walk with Him. She came to love the Word of God and to love being with His people and serving in ways that she could. There was no more going back, feeling the old shame over and over, and reviewing her wounds. She became a woman free from the bondage of the past.

But before this process of healing was as far along as it would ultimately be, Mary still struggled with certain issues. One of the greatest things that grieved her was what she considered to be the utter waste of her life. She surrendered her life to Christ when she was sixty-two years old—and she regarded all that had happened prior to that as a complete loss, filled with sin and rebellion and terrible decisions. Having seen truth and light, it was hard for her to see how she could have been so foolish. So she periodically beat herself up with sorrow and guilt. This, of course, was the work of Satan, who had lost her but was still determined to do as much damage as possible to sabotage her life.

It was on one of these occasions, when we sat at the kitchen table, having coffee, studying the scripture, and sharing, that the Lord provided a breakthrough for Mary. She had broken down weeping, thinking again about the loss of so much of her life. It seemed that her tears were endless; I had never known anyone as deeply wounded as Mary. As always, we prayed together, asking God to move her from these sorrowful regrets and bring her fully into her new life in Christ. After praying, Mary always felt better, so she hugged me as she was leaving, and we planned to meet again the following morning, as was our custom.

Now it happened that during part of this period of my friendship with Mary, we were very blessed to have two young missionaries from India staying with us as they waited for their visas to enter their assigned country. The visas were delayed for quite some time, so they had become well acquainted with Mary and were also an important part of discipling her in her Christian growth.

On this particular morning, as Mary and I were in the kitchen having coffee, Rob and Shini were upstairs in their room, having a time of prayer. They did not see Mary that morning and only came down after she had gone home. But when they did come down, they mentioned that they had felt led to pray for Mary that morning and that the Lord had given them a word for her. The Word was from Joel 2:25

> "I will restore to you the years that the swarming locust
> has eaten,"

Imagine the feeling of hearing these perfect words of encouragement! And imagine the reaction of Mary when Shini called her and told her what the Lord had spoken to them that very day! It was another round of tears, but this time, they were tears of hope and tears of amazement that the Lord loved her so much as to send her such specific words from Him. It was the last time I ever heard Mary mourn about her lost years.

The Mary Stories
Part 5: Good-Bye, Sister

$\mathcal{A}$s Mary and I sat drinking coffee at my kitchen table one cold morning, she told me a story about her brother so astonishing in its import that it brought me to tears. I had the great privilege of interpreting this story to her to show her its greater meaning; subsequently, it became a story of victory and not defeat—and the day became an extraordinary one for both of us.

Mary had been a raging alcoholic for most of her adult years, as I've shared. Although she had been delivered from the unbearable guilt and sorrow that had consumed most of her life, there were still times when she recalled specific incidents that she very much regretted. She would share these stories with me at times, and we would pray for the Lord to specifically forgive her and then give her victory over the returning thoughts about things that could not be changed.

One of the things Mary learned as she came to know her Savior better and better is that He had been with her through all her lost years. He had been the Hand of protection over her. He had put things in place for her to look back and see with great joy; for He knew that she would one day belong to Him and He would bring forth these blessings even from her darkest hours.

One of these blessings turned out to be a memory of her brother. Mary came from a family where no love and nurturing had occurred. She and her brother and sister had no memory of as much as a hug throughout their childhood. They were all unloved and unwanted. It was a shameful story of neglect and abuse, and all these children were badly damaged. Her brother spent most of his adult life in prison. Mary had minimal contact with him over the years, and being so absorbed with her own devastated life, she had virtually no concern for anyone else, including her brother. But, once saved, she shared with me this story about her brother, probably because there was something still troubling about it.

One day, as Mary sat watching TV and drinking as usual, she received a call from her brother, then out of prison and trying to make it in the world. She was annoyed to even hear his voice. The siblings tended to shun one another, since any contact made them all think of their horrible past. So for this reason, and also because she was more or less drunk and simply did not want her program to be interrupted, Mary was very little engaged with this conversation from her brother. However, he said something so odd that it caused her to pay a little more attention.

"Mary," he said, "I have called to say good-bye to you because I am soon going to die."

"What's the matter with you? Are you sick?"

"No, I'm not sick, but I know for certain that I'm going to die, and it's really all right. I just wanted to say good-bye to you."

"How the h--- do you know you are going to die?" said the then foul-mouthed Mary, now thoroughly irritated at having her attention so drawn away from her program and her liquor.

"I know because Jesus told me it was going to happen. I had a dream where Jesus spoke to me. I never knew Him, Mary, but he talked to me—just like you and I are talking now—and He told me that my time to die was very soon. He told me He would take me Home to be with

Him and would forgive all my sins if I would trust in Him. I do, Mary, I do trust Him. He is God! I'm going to be with Him soon. Good-bye, Mary. I love you."

The conversation ended. Mary was stunned by what he said, so much so that the memory of his words lingered through the years. It was especially lodged forever in her mind because, three days later, she got word that her brother had died.

Now, a great many years later, Mary herself had come to know Jesus as her Savior. On this particular day, Mary looked back with great sadness at her indifference to her brother in their last conversation.

But I saw immediately the gravity of what she had shared and finally managed to tearfully say to her, "Mary, do you know what this means? Your brother will be waiting for you in heaven! He has also been saved!"

Somehow, in the newness of her walk with the Lord, Mary had not put this together. But then she realized—of course it was true! Her brother had met Jesus and was saved all those many years ago. And in the gracious manner of a Loving Father, the Lord had gotten word to Mary so that she could rejoice in this knowledge after she also came to trust in Him years later.

We two friends wept together, greatly humbled and praising God for His unspeakable mercy to the two outcast siblings who had never been loved before they met Jesus.

The Mary Stories
Part 6: A Neighbor Who Prayed

After she came to know Jesus in a personal and saving way, Mary began to see her past in a different light altogether. She began to see how God had been the Hound of Heaven, patiently following her over the years—and creating situations that she would someday understand.

One of the things in her past that Mary remembered was something she had considered totally odd at the time. For a period of time, she had lived next door to a very kind woman who seemed genuinely concerned for her. The woman tried to befriend her, but Mary rejected all her efforts, being completely absorbed in her alcoholic life and keeping everyone at arm's length. But because the woman was so persistent, Mary always looked back and remembered her kindly—even as she considered her to be strange.

Her last memory of the woman came on the day she was moving away from the area. The neighbor came over to say good-bye as the moving truck was loading Mary's things. She treated Mary as if they were truly friends, in spite of Mary's rebuffs of her attempts at friendship. But in this last meeting they would ever have, the neighbor hugged Mary and made a comment to her that Mary had not the slightest possibility of understanding. But neither could she forget it. As Mary recalled, the woman said, "Mary, the Lord has shown me that you will have a life like Mary Magdalene's. Like her, you will find your way to know Jesus. I will be praying for you in the days ahead."

Mary confessed to me that she had no idea what this meant but had a vague suspicion that it was some kind of biblical reference—especially since the neighbor was always talking to her about God. Once again, I was stunned by this revelation, for by this time, I knew a great deal of Mary's story. She had been married five times, for example, along with many other indications of the kind of life she had lived. I sat speechless for a few seconds as I considered the obvious fact that God had given this neighbor of long ago a prophetic word and had called her to prayer for a lost woman who would hardly give her the time of day.

When I recovered from the lump in my throat, I told Mary that the general belief about Mary Magdalene of the Bible was that she had led an impure life before she met Jesus; but in the final count, she was redeemed from her past and ultimately became a faithful servant, following Jesus to the cross and then having the privilege of being one of the first to see her Lord resurrected. "A great story of redemption," I told Mary.

Mary and I sat in quiet amazement. We both clearly understood how God had placed markers in her life that would later show her He had been there all along. I then gave Mary a copy of Francis Thompson's immortal poem "The Hound of Heaven." She realized that she had been long pursued by her Lord.

The Mary Stories
Part 7: Casting Off Time

$\mathcal{A}$lthough Mary and I were good friends for many years, our backgrounds were polar opposites. She was from Brooklyn, New York; I was from Alabama. She was from a loveless family who left her broken and shamed; I was from a family who loved and cared for me. She rejected God at an early age; I came to know God at an early age. The list went on and on. The differences between us were great in most every respect; nevertheless, we would both testify that we "had all things in common." We had all things in common because of our bond in Christ. We were fellow sinners, fellow strugglers, and fellow believers. All other differences simply did not matter.

For several years, Mary and I were neighbors. As described, this was how we became the best of friends, sharing our stories at my kitchen table, where, through Jesus, Mary began to heal from the terrible wounds of her past. This was where we both grew in our knowledge and love of the Lord, and where we witnessed together the incredible, personal ways that He called us both to a deeper walk with Him.

It was a special season for us both. It was special for Mary because she came to know Jesus Christ in a very personal and saving way. Her entire life did an about-face; she discovered for the first time what it was to have peace of soul. It was special for me because I saw, up close and personal, the incredible ways that God reached out to Mary. I saw the endless "coincidences" of His moving directly in her life—to show her very specific things, first and foremost, His unconditional love. I will never forget the numerous times when the Lord's messages to Mary and His obvious love for her came about in such unique ways that it was stunning to see—and a great faith builder for me as well.

Mary was a highly intelligent person and not especially willing to believe something without evidence. But how many times did Mary, the once atheist and doubter supreme say to me, "This *cannot* be coincidence! There *is* a God, and He has set His sights on me!"

So these years as neighbors were good ones. But, of course, we all know that change is inevitable. So it was that we both moved to other cities, other states, and the morning coffee and fellowship ended. These were sad times for us both. I was concerned that Mary would find it difficult to connect with Christians in her new city. She might revert to her tendency to be isolated. She might not be ready to persevere on her own. Such little faith on my part! For God knows the state of each of us, and He knew Mary belonged to Him always and forever. He knew she would never fall back.

Indeed, Mary did make her way in the new setting. She sought out Christian fellowship with the zeal that she once had in seeking multiple recovery meetings. She seemed to be involved in some way in multiple churches in her new area. I would laugh to hear her stories of the various Bible studies she attended and the events she found to participate in within the Christian community. She continued to read and study the scripture until she was as familiar with it as if she had studied her entire life. This was a very long way from the time when she had only studied one chapter in the entire Bible and was ashamed to show up in church with such little knowledge.

So our friendship continued by phone. I only saw her one more time face-to-face after we went our separate ways, but how we loved to catch up by phone! She still had many struggles, especially with the knowledge of unsaved family members, and she tried endlessly to be a witness to them as to the power of God. Certainly they were able to see the total change in her own life. Another challenge during this period when we were separated geographically was the death of her husband. But even in this, dear Mary, once so unstable, bore up under the challenge and continued forward victoriously with the help of her Lord. Her faith never wavered, and she was always "just realizing" something new in her walk with God.

Mary and I occasionally had a conversation in regard to heaven. She would say, "I just find it hard to believe that we can have all these incredible blessings in this life and then go to an even better place to be with God. It's just too good to be true." Now Mary was not a doubter of the Word of God, but somehow she thought there must be something we were not understanding in this. Simply put, she wondered how these great things could come to such a sinner as she. She still had a certain sense of her unworthiness at times, and she could not fathom such rewards in the face of what her life had been. Mary was definitely more in the camp of

"God, be merciful to me, a sinner!" (Luke 18:13)

than she was in the camp of

"God, I thank You that I'm not like other men," (Luke 18:11).

In these conversations, I would always just say, "Well, Mary, someday you will see Jesus face-to-face—and then you will know."

This and other conversations would often reveal Mary's true humility, which was one of many things the Lord showed me in great depth through my association with Mary. I had guided her through her very first chapter of the Bible, but she ultimately became a much greater teacher to me, showing me truths of God I will never forget.

One of the most unusual things I remember about Mary is that she did not want to receive compliments. This was not just false or even honest modesty. She was *afraid* of compliments, and she asked me in all sincerity to not hand them out to her. It was all very well if I pointed out how *the Lord* was at work in her life; in this she fairly beamed. But I was to lay nothing to her credit. She explained this aversion by telling me that she had spent a lifetime being a very needy person and trying to elevate herself by her own arrogance. Rejected people, she told me, can quickly rush to pride. After all, she knew what the Bible said, that a person is tested by the praise he or she receives. And she never believed she was strong enough to withstand compliments. I have to say that this, along with many other insights from Mary, were unlike anything I had ever before considered—and I was much the richer for her having taught me these things.

The day came when Mary called me to say she was ill. She had been having a hard time breathing, she had gone to the doctor She received a diagnosis of lung cancer. Mary had been a smoker for many years, only breaking the habit after she became a Christian. She did not know what to expect from this diagnosis, but I could tell that it was serious and very well advanced from what she told me. An amazing thing happened before she was hospitalized. One of her sons, perhaps the one for whom she was the most concerned, stayed at her house to help her in every way possible. He had a calming effect on her, and their past stormy relationship settled into a very different place.

During this first conversation when Mary told me about her condition, we prayed together, emphasizing that she would not be afraid and would trust God in everything. As it turned out, the disease advanced very rapidly, and we only spoke two more times before her final hospitalization.

A call came from a Christian friend of Mary's. She told me Mary was in the hospital again and would probably not live much longer. With all the courage I could muster, I called Mary in the hospital to say good-bye. It was so hard to think of this parting, temporary though I knew it was to be. She answered the phone and was still able to talk, but with some difficulty. She enthusiastically called my name, and we immediately began to talk about our favorite subject: Jesus. Neither of us pretended she was not dying, for we had practiced brutal honesty with one another over many years.

"Mary," I said to her, "it looks like you will see Jesus before I do. And then you will know that heaven is not too good to be true. You will see the sights and hear the sounds—just as the Apostle Paul said

> "What no eye has seen, nor ear heard, nor the heart of
> man imagined, what God has prepared for those who
> love him"
>   (1 Corinthians 2:9)

And when we meet again, I will say, 'I told you so.'"

With a great deal of effort, Mary managed to breathe out enthusiastically, "Oh, I believe you now, dear friend, I believe you now—with all my heart! Good-bye until I see you *there*. I love you."

"Yes, Mary, see you *there!* I love you too."

Morning Prayer

O Lord, we awaken from the night's sleep,
    and there is a fleeting moment of consciousness
    without remembrance—
        a moment when we are not yet hammered
        by the boulder of our circumstances.

But then, the knowledge of good and evil floods over us,
    as we remember our human dilemma.
You told our ancient parents to leave the one tree alone—
    the one that gave us options to choose the dark path;
        they did not listen and
        we have not listened—
        and now the fruit we have eaten is too bitter to bear.

So as the full power of our minds
    is brutally snapped on once again,
    and we face the reality of overwhelming evil
        for yet another day,
        we pray that we will not stop
            to think on this brutality;
            that we not allow our faithless, rebellious minds
                to serve us up with messages
                of futility, self-hatred, or bitterness toward others.

We pray that today we will not devise ridiculous schemes
    to put the world back aright by our own plans,
    to manage the unmanageable,
    to put mere Band-Aids on mountains of pain …
        or to suck a tiny moment of relief
        from some sinful plot we will devise—
            which will only make the mountain greater

and call forth The Dragon from his cave,
with teeth sharpened to devour us.

Let us not insist, against all sanity,
that we have strength of our own,
that our own plans, which *have not worked* in the past,
will now work—
And let us not prevent wisdom from overtaking us
by our many diversions, preventing *real help*.

But for today, Lord, when we awake
and have the split second of reprieve
before we remember again that we live near the Dragon,
with all that is within us, let us praise You!
And when the full surge of awareness powers on,
with all the urgency of a soldier awaking to war,
knowing the enemy has encircled us, is among us,
and before our emotions can flood our beings with fear—
let us speak to You, who has absolute authority
over the Dragon.

"Good morning, Captain of the Hosts!"
Isn't it true that *Your* Army
is present in this dangerous place?
Have we failed to see this spectacular sight?
Aren't these the legions of angels and flaming hosts
that were once revealed to the servant of Elisha,
and that caused him to tremble with fear?

Would You then, O Lord, draw our minds to what we *know*,
before the shipwreck of our emotions can take us down.
Would You O Lord, refresh us, renew us, and remind us
through the authority and power of Your written revelation—
Would You, O Lord, lift us upward to the Real and the True,

and take our hearts and minds into the heavenly regions
    where Your glory is always on display.

And then, O Lord, return us to the assignment for *this* day,
    filled with the Truth, armed with the Big Picture,
        peace restored, minds and hearts aligned once more
        with the Narrow Way,
            knowing our destiny,
                determined to make it Home,
                    not crawling over the finish line,
                        but running to the end—
                            with the inexplicable joy
                                which comes with knowing The Real You.

And with the fresh determination
        to glorify Your Name
            On earth as it is in heaven.

Morning of Glory

A wordless memory of long ago still paints an exquisite picture for an aging mind. It floats to the surface of consciousness for an occasional visit, always bringing impressions and feelings that have remained without definition for many decades, and always pouring out some nameless joy and unspeakable comfort. Now it is time to form the words and plumb the depths of early meaning.

It was in the cool of the early morning, maybe summer or maybe spring. A father held his very young daughter in his arms and took her to the garden fence. Vegetables were growing inside the fence; sticks were in the ground, with vines climbing skyward; green leaves sparkled freshly in rows along the ground, beginning to show their various gifts of food. The very feel of this long-ago morning has lingered over the years—the fresh, unused air of the day; the dew still shining on the plants; the look of the rustic wooden fence posts, placed at intervals to support rectangular-shaped wire fencing.

But these lovely scenes were just the background setting for the most magical, mystical picture of all—a cluster of morning glories which had assembled themselves on the garden fence above the crawling vegetables. They seemed to have been born on the very corner post, as they traveled gloriously in both directions, winding gracefully with hope of totally framing the blessings of food beneath. They were wondrous in their beauty, displaying a heavenly blue color—as if part of the sky had been borrowed for their creation.

No memory of particular words from the father was ever recalled from that morning, but new thoughts were forever formed in the mind of the child. From that day forward, the child knew that morning glories went to sleep every night, just as children do. And she knew that each morning they were awakened by the great shining sun. They slept with their petals closed and opened their petal eyes when the sun beckoned them to do so. It was all so incredible—the best story ever. The sun, so far away, would reach to the garden fence morning after morning, alerting the delicate little flowers to begin their day.

There is another layer of this memory, also not attached to any recalled words. From this scene came a certainty in the heart of the child that the great sun and the beautiful morning glories were doing the bidding of a much Greater Master—Someone mightier and brighter than the sun, and more glorious than the heavenly blue morning glories—Someone unspeakably good. A holy and awesome reverence is always the attendant to this visiting memory.

The father must have used his wisest words to paint this picture so profoundly that it has lasted a lifetime, still producing fruit in the old age of the former child. The snapshot memory remains an indelible image, a display of ultimate Truth—always filled with the comfort and hope that accompanies Truth.

Perhaps there will be another garden fence in God's own paradise, a fence where the morning glories of heaven are beyond anything we have seen, and the air fresher than the freshest morning we have known—with the light so dazzling that we will know we are in the presence of the Son of God, the Master and Maker of the beckoning sun and the beautiful morning glories. And waiting, of course, will be the earthly father who pointed the child to the Heavenly Father.

A Closing Word to the Reader

$\mathcal{S}$ometimes we tend to look at the stories and lives of others and wonder why we have not seen such happenings in our own lives. I want to address this by describing a few things we need to consider. First and foremost, we must look closer and learn to pay attention to the blessings that God continually grants each of us in great and small ways. There are daily stories happening in our lives as God's people—if we have eyes to see. Perhaps, to a certain extent, we take for granted the ordinary occurrences in our lives, and, consequently, we fail to recognize His hand. We might thank God for every time we survive interstate travel and arrive safely at home, for example. Or for every day that we do not go hungry.

The next point is to observe great caution in today's world, as there is danger in having a cultural view of God and thereby believing things that are not true of Him. He is not Santa Claus, standing by to grant our wishes. This tends to be the general view, even in churches sometimes. He has not promised us a life of ease. Jesus Himself said that in this world we would have trouble. When trouble comes, then, are we to fall away since God is not living up to our expectations?

In addition, in order to really experience the daily blessings and see the incredible ways that God interacts with us, we must know Him on a personal basis, on a saving basis. We must accept in totality what the Bible says about the way God has reached out to us to reveal Himself through the life and testimony of Jesus Christ who was God among us, showing us the nature and character of who He is and how we are to be reconciled to a Holy God, even though we are great sinners. To trust Him to forgive us, because He took our sins on Himself through His brutal death on a cross. To truly repent and commit to a new life following Him—for this begins a transformed life for all of us. We must remember, though, that it does not begin an easy life, but a blessed life, a life in which we can be assured that all things that happen, good or bad, can be turned to glorify God through the ways we respond to both trials and victories. And God will show us that even out of the ashes of tragedy, He brings redemption in incredible ways that will serve for our greatest good.

We must also have no doubt that God also reaches out to those who do not know Him. He is the Hound of Heaven, tracking our steps through dark places, always inviting us to come to the Light. The Bible tells us that His mercy is shown to us while we are yet sinners. He does not wait on us to call on Him; He continually calls on us at all times.

Finally, as we take seriously our daily walk with God, we should pay very great attention. We will indeed begin to tell the stories of our own unique history with God.